SWIMMING
WILD
IN SCOTLAND

SWIMMING WILD IN SCOTLAND

A GUIDE TO OVER 100 SCOTTISH RIVER, LOCH AND SEA SWIMMING SPOTS

ALICE GOODRIDGE

Vertebrate Publishing, Sheffield
www.adventurebooks.com

SWIMMING WILD IN SCOTLAND

A GUIDE TO OVER 100 SCOTTISH RIVER, LOCH AND SEA SWIMMING SPOTS

First published in 2023 by Vertebrate Publishing. Reprinted in 2024.

VERTEBRATE PUBLISHING
Omega Court, 352 Cemetery Road, Sheffield S11 8FT, United Kingdom.
www.adventurebooks.com

ISBN 978-1-83981-176-0 (Paperback)
ISBN 978-1-83981-177-7 (Ebook)

Front cover: Seagull Island, Loch Leven © Vivien Cumming.
Back cover: L–R: St Mary's Loch © Grahame Connor; Upper Loch Torridon; Pattack Falls © Becca Harvey; Swimmers salute; Coll © Alastair Goodridge; River Etive © Alastair Goodridge; Seamill Beach © Kiara Henderson; Coilleag a' Phrionnsa, Eriskay.
Photography by Alice Goodridge unless otherwise credited.

Swimming location maps reproduced by permission of Ordnance Survey on behalf of The Controller of Her Majesty's Stationery Office. © Crown Copyright. 100025218.

Regional maps created by Lovell Johns Ltd. Contains OS data © Crown copyright and database right 2023. www.lovelljohns.com

Scotland overview map by Active Maps. www.activemaps.co.uk

Edited by Helen Parry, design and production by Jane Beagley.
www.adventurebooks.com

Swimming Wild book series created by Suzanna Cruickshank, author of *Swimming Wild in the Lake District*.
www.suzannaswims.co.uk

Printed and bound in Slovenia by Latitude Press.

Vertebrate Publishing is committed to printing on paper from sustainable sources.

Opposite Triple Falls above the Triangle Pool, **River Etive** © Vivien Cumming

Key

1 **Argyll & the Isles**
2 **Skye & Lochaber**
3 **Outer Hebrides**
4 **North-West Mainland**
5 **Far North**
6 **Central Highlands**
7 **The East**
8 **Perthshire, Loch Lomond & the Trossachs**
9 **Central & Southern Scotland**

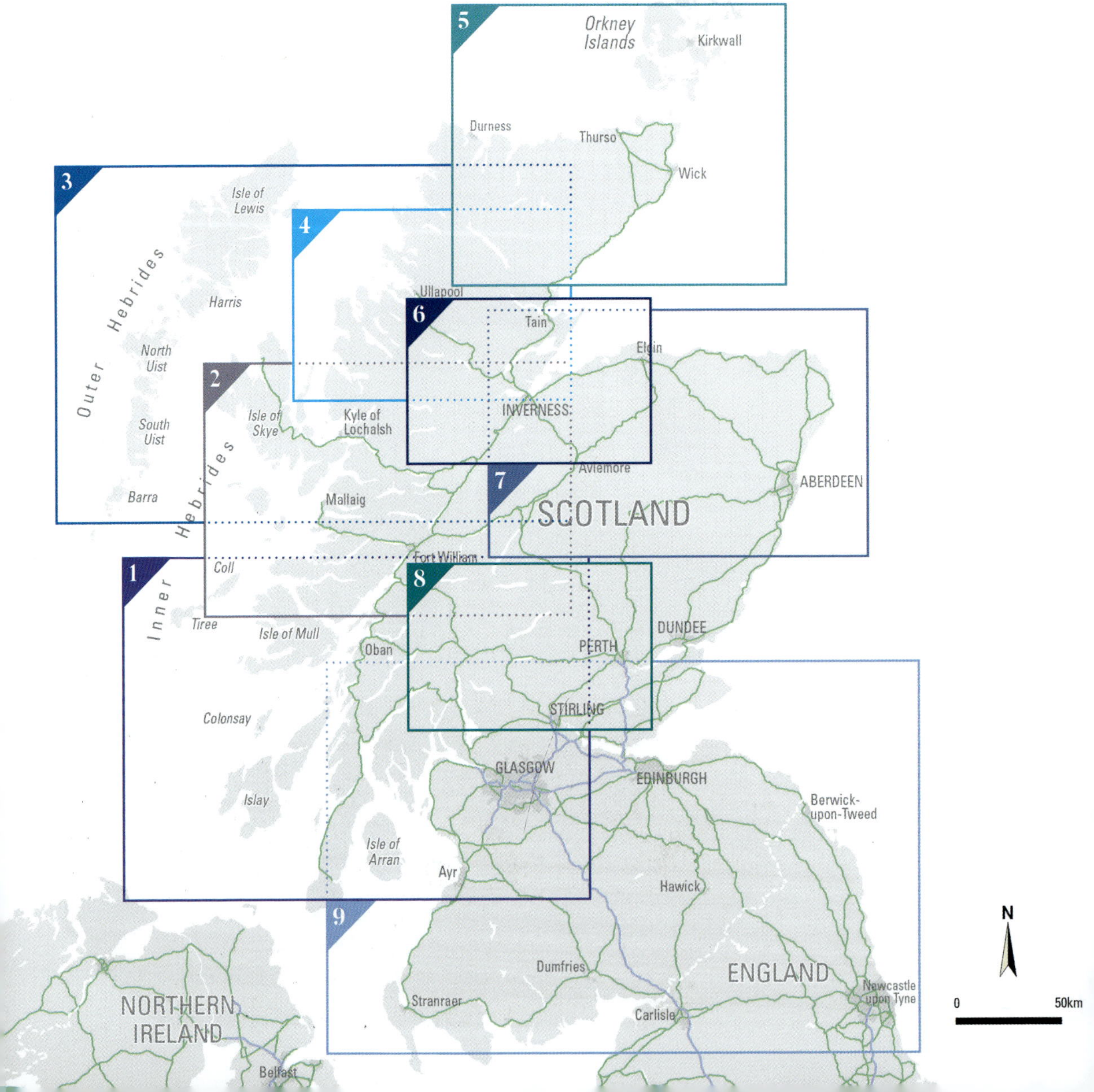

Opposite The author exploring tidal pools on Coll © Alastair Goodridge

Introduction

Swimming has been a part of my life for as long as I can remember. Starting in the pool, I switched to open water over a decade ago and have never looked back. Now I swim outside almost every day, all year round, whatever the weather.

Since moving to the Scottish Highlands in 2013, my love of swimming has been my route to exploring Scotland's watery landscape. Starting close to home in the Cairngorms National Park, I've swum my way around local lochs, circumnavigated castles, swooshed along rivers and ventured up into the hills to dip in remote mountain lochs and waterfalls.

Further afield, I've been lucky enough to lead multiple swimming expeditions around Skye, the Small Isles, the Outer Hebrides and St Kilda. I've explored the remote Ardnamurchan and Knoydart peninsulas, visited friends to dip around the coast of Orkney and travelled to Unst – one of the Shetland Islands – to swim at the most northerly beach in the UK.

Along the way, I have completed solo swims of the length of two of Scotland's largest freshwater lochs – Loch Lomond (the largest by surface area) and Loch Awe (the longest). I've also swum the length of Loch Ness (the largest by volume) as part of a relay team and guided many people swimming in Loch Morar, Scotland's deepest loch.

After many years of being asked to recommend places to swim around Scotland, I thought that a guidebook would be extremely useful. A proper guidebook with maps that show people exactly where to get into the water. A guidebook that included lots of useful location-specific information, written by someone who had swum there. A guidebook that (very importantly) provided plenty of local post-swim refreshment options. I should sit down and write one.

I soon realised I was too busy leading swimming expeditions, organising events and running swimming workshops. I concluded that I didn't have the time and pushed the idea to the back of my mind. Fast-forward to a global pandemic, and I finally had a moment to sit down and make a plan. The guidebook was back on, and I set off to visit many familiar and new swimming spots all over Scotland's mainland and islands.

This book is by no means an exhaustive guide to every possible swimming location around Scotland. It just touches the surface, highlighting some of the best places to swim around the country. I have endless notes, photographs and enough information to include thousands of swimming spots but, alas, the final cut had to be limited. Over 100 swimming spots are included; it is a selection based on multiple criteria, taking into account my swimming experiences, geographical location, variety, accessibility and infrastructure.

Most of all, I have loved swimming in every place I have included in this book, all for different reasons. I hope you enjoy them too.

Happy swimming!

Access rights & wild swimming in Scotland

Scotland is a wild swimmer's paradise, as long as you like cold water! There are over 25,000 freshwater lochs and lochans, along with more than 125,000 kilometres of rivers and streams, varying from deep, wide Lowland rivers to small Highland burns. There are also around 18,000 kilometres of coastline (including numerous sea lochs). With so much water, we are certainly spoilt for choice when it comes to swimming.

When Scottish legislation on public access rights changed in 2003, it marked the moment when the lands and waters of Scotland became open to anyone who wanted to explore them for recreational and educational purposes. The Scottish Outdoor Access Code legally allows us the 'right to roam' – and swim – without restrictions, as long as we do so responsibly.

The Scottish Outdoor Access Code is based on three key principles:

» Take responsibility for your own actions.
» Respect the interests of others.
» Care for the environment.

So, with all this freedom, we can literally swim anywhere, right? Well, not exactly. Not all bodies of water are swimmable or safe. There are also a few common-sense exceptions, including access through people's gardens, farmyards, airfields and land used for military activities.

We must swim responsibly and recognise that swimming in cold water can be a potentially dangerous activity. In other areas of the UK, inland waterways often have restricted access, with either no swimming, or paid-for swimming only. Having the freedom to roam and swim is a privilege we should never take for granted. Always leave no trace, pick up litter and try to leave your swimming spot better than you found it.

The Scottish Outdoor Access Code for swimmers

When in the water

» Never swim close to reservoir structures, water intakes, abstraction points, spillways or weirs.
» Avoid fishing nets or other fishing tackle.
» Do not disturb anglers and other water users – cooperate and be considerate.
» Always acknowledge considerate behaviour by other water users – be polite.
» Do not pollute the water – it may be used for a public water supply.
» Keep noise to a minimum.

When accessing the water

» Take care not to disturb livestock.
» Take extra care to prevent damage to sensitive natural habitats. In coastal areas, follow any local guidance aimed at reducing dune or machair erosion.
» Avoid disturbing sensitive birds and animals, particularly during the nesting and breeding season.
» Respect people's privacy and peace of mind – access rights do not extend to people's gardens.
» Avoid damage to fences, gates, crops, vegetation and riverbanks at water access points.
» Be considerate when parking – never block tracks or obstruct entrances to fields or buildings.

For further information, go to
www.outdooraccess-scotland.scot

1 Synchronised splashing, Sanna Bay

How to get started

The first step can be the hardest, as we often find a multitude of reasons why we will start something tomorrow or next week rather than today.

FIND SOMEONE TO SWIM WITH

Finding a local swimming group near where you live or where you are visiting is a good place to start. These are generally informal groups for making social arrangements to swim. The collective local knowledge of these groups is often invaluable. They'll know the best and safest places to get in the water and have their own routines, which you can learn from. Even if you are not a 'group' kind of person, they are a good place to start to help you find one or two other people to share your swims with.

There is a list of UK outdoor swimming groups on the Outdoor Swimming Society's website, which includes some of the more established Scottish groups: *www.outdoor swimmingsociety.com* In addition, many smaller groups have been created in the last few years all around Scotland; Facebook can be a good place to search for local groups. For swimming locations in this book, I have provided inform-ation on local swimming groups where possible.

If you don't fancy joining a group, or you can't find one locally, maybe you have a friend you can persuade to join you for a dip. For safety reasons, it is really important that you do not swim alone. At the very least, you need to find someone willing to keep a close eye on you while you dip or swim parallel to the shore.

If you would like more guidance, find a qualified open water swimming coach and book a group or one-to-one lesson – many run introductory sessions for beginners. There are also a growing number of qualified swimming guides who provide safety cover and guidance to help you explore an area safely.

START SMALL

If you are used to swimming a certain distance in the pool, you will likely have to reduce this considerably when swimming in cold water. Don't be tempted to tackle a 500-metre loop the first time you get in the water. Instead, start with a few quick dips – they will help you get used to the new environment and start to

deal with the cold. If possible, choose calm conditions on a sunny day for your first swim – anything that makes it a little less daunting.

But how quick is a quick dip? Start by doing a few strokes once your shoulders are under the water; maybe stay in for a couple of minutes, then get out. That's it! All over in less than five minutes. If you are wearing a wetsuit, you may want to stay in for a bit longer, but still, keep it short. You may not want to get out of the water at this point but get out anyway. The practice of getting ready for your swim and dressed afterwards (arguably the most challenging part – the swimming part will feel quite easy in comparison) will be well worth it. Hopefully you will enjoy your swim and come back wanting more.

After your first couple of dips, you can start extending your swims gradually. You will still be learning how your body copes with cold water immersion and open water conditions, so don't be tempted to increase your time or distance in the water too rapidly. I find a simple waterproof watch with a stopwatch function helps me to keep track of my time in the water. Of course, if you want to stick with quick dips, that's fine too.

BE PREPARED

A successful and enjoyable swim or dip is all in the planning. I often spend more time preparing for a swim than I do in the water – especially in the winter when swims are brief, but risks are higher.

I tend to break my swim into several parts: before (at home and at the side of the water), getting in, during and after. Get all these stages right and you are likely to have a wonderful experience and leave wrapped up warm in your many layers, excited to plan your next dip. Get one of these stages wrong and you could have a miserable experience and never want to swim outside again.

Before leaving home

Do your homework. Research, plan and prepare. For the swimming spots in this book, I have provided as much location-specific information as possible. However, you will still always need to check variable factors on the day, such as weather, wind, tides and sea state, to assess whether it is safe to enter the water. Check the weather forecast, including wind direction and speed. Is your chosen swimming spot likely to be exposed or sheltered? If it is forecast to be very windy, are there more sheltered places to swim nearby? If it's likely to be raining, do you have a plan for keeping your post-swim kit dry? What will the access be like – might it be muddy, flooded or a long walk away at low tide? For river swims, are the water levels safe? For coastal locations, how big are the waves? When is slack tide?

Read the appropriate safety section of this book so you are familiar with the particular things you need to consider when you're planning freshwater loch swims (pages xxi–xxii), swims in rivers and waterfalls (pages xxiii–xxiv) and swims in the sea (pages xxiv–xxvii).

Who are you swimming with? Make arrangements – exactly where are you going to meet? Try to never swim alone. If you can't find someone to come in the water with you, who will keep an eye on you from the shore?

Pack your bag (see pages xvii–xx for information on equipment). Don't forget to take lots of warm layers for afterwards, even if it's a relatively warm day. If you are ever wondering if you have enough layers, take more!

Fuel up. Swimming in cold water and warming up afterwards uses up lots of energy. Ensure you have had enough to eat and are well hydrated before swimming. Pack pre- and post-swim snacks. Boil the kettle and fill up your flask so you have a nice hot drink for afterwards – hot chocolate, ginger tea or hot berry squash, whatever takes your fancy.

Don't drink and drown. Alcohol, drugs and cold water do not mix well. Alcohol lowers your perception of risk and hinders your body's ability to regulate temperature. It is never a good idea: just don't do it.

Have an emergency plan (see page xvi). Make sure your phone is fully charged.

Before you get in the water

Is it safe? You've done all your homework, identified a good place to swim, and you may have driven for an hour to get there, but you won't know whether it is actually safe to swim until you have seen the conditions for yourself. Hopefully, it will look wonderful and inviting, and you can get on with your swim. But if it is too exposed, flowing too fast, the waves are too big or you just don't feel it's safe to swim – *don't get in* (and don't let anyone persuade you otherwise).

Check your entry and exit points. Where is the best place to get in and out? Is it a gently sloping entry, or does it get deep quickly? Exit points should be as easy as possible. Climbing or scrambling out over rocks may be easy when you are warm and full of energy, but it can become impossible if you get too cold and have lost some of your coordination.

Organise your post-swim kit. Pile your clothes up with the first things you will need when you get out of the water easily accessible on the top of the pile. I always ensure my woolly hat is on the top, then my towel, and then layers for my top half. Being organised can make all the difference to getting dressed quickly after a swim.

Leaving your kit. I normally leave my kit bag visible on the shore, but I occasionally tuck it behind a rock or camouflage it. I'm usually more worried about a hungry Labrador stealing my snacks or a dog peeing on my bag than someone stealing my clothes! If you are concerned about leaving your valuables, you can put them inside your tow float. Always put them inside an additional watertight dry bag to ensure they won't get wet.

Getting in

No matter how often you swim outdoors, you will always feel the initial shock of the cold as you get into the water because the temperature of the water is much colder than your body temperature.

Get in slowly. *Never* jump or dive straight in. Cold water shock is extremely dangerous and can be fatal. Enter the water gradually. Splash water on your arms, across your shoulders and around your face and neck so that the contrast of temperature isn't such a shock when you fully submerge. If you are wearing a wetsuit, allow some water in (at the neck) when you are ready for it, rather than waiting for the cold to suddenly flood in and hit you when you are not expecting it.

Exhale. Instinct tells us to take a massive breath in and hold it when the cold hits, or to gasp and take lots of shallow breaths in. Remember to breathe out. Singing, shrieking or swearing are all acceptable at this stage, as they mean you are exhaling and definitely not holding your breath.

It's not a race. Set off gently. Start with some relaxed head-up breaststroke before considering putting your face in the water. Keep focusing on exhaling until your breathing has settled. After a couple of minutes, the water will feel lovely, and you will wonder what all the fuss was about.

During your swim

Be aware of other water users. Avoid swimming in areas with boat traffic, and make sure you are as visible as possible in the water. Wear a brightly coloured hat and use a tow float. Never assume someone has seen you, however visible you think you are – they are not necessarily expecting to see swimmers in the water. If a boat is approaching and doesn't seem to have noticed you, wave your tow float above your head to attract their attention. If you plan to do a longer swim, consider finding someone who can kayak or paddleboard next to you.

Know your own limits. Be sensible. Don't swim out into the middle of the loch or overestimate your ability. That rock – or island – may look as if it is close by, but it is likely to be a lot further away than you think, and then you have to swim back again. Stick close to the shore and swim parallel to the shoreline so you can easily get out as soon as you need to. If you're with a group who are more experienced, it's easy to accidentally stay in for longer than you intended. Don't be afraid to say, 'I'm just going to have a quick dip and then get out' or 'I'm not going out of my depth today'. Keep to your plan, and don't feel pressured into going further than you are comfortable with.

Cramp. If you get a cramp while swimming, stop and rest on your tow float and try to stretch it out. If it is really bad, signal to someone to come and help you.

Get out wanting more. Knowing when to get out is a tricky business. Everyone is different, and experience is the best teacher. Short dips are the best way to start, very gradually building up your time in the water as you get to know how your body feels during each swim, and how it recovers afterwards. Your temperature will continue to drop long after you get out of the water, so you need to get out before you start feeling too cold. Feel like you could happily stay in the water for another five minutes? Don't wait five minutes – *get out now*.

Don't get too cold. Hypothermia is a real risk. If your teeth start to chatter, you feel lightheaded or your limbs start feeling heavy in the water, making swimming hard work, you have already stayed in for too long. Get out ASAP and make sure there is someone to help you afterwards.

It is worth noting that your ability to cope with the cold will differ from one swim to the next. Whether it is external factors like air temperature, water temperature or wind chill,

or personal factors like lack of sleep, lack of energy (food) or starting new medication, just because you stayed in the water for a certain amount of time yesterday, it doesn't mean you should do the same or more today.

Keep an eye on other swimmers. If someone looks like they are struggling, go over and see if you can help. They might have a problem with leaking goggles, they might have cramp or be feeling panicky in the water. If the other person is visibly shivering, confused, slowing down or mumbling their words, it's likely that they are getting too cold, and you should accompany them out of the water (even if you were planning a longer swim) and make sure they get warm as soon as possible.

Afterwards

Don't hang around. You may feel fantastic when you get out of the water, but now is not the time for faffing! Your core body temperature will continue to drop once you get out of the water and will be coldest between 15 and 40 minutes after your swim. This is called *afterdrop*. Wind chill exacerbates this. You've got a five-to-ten-minute window to get all your clothes on before the cold hits you and shivers kick in, so make the most of it and get dressed as quickly as you can. It's much harder to do up zips when your hands are shaking!

Cover up and get dry. I always put on my woolly hat first (over my silicone swimming hat), then a towelling robe or anything to keep the wind off. Get that wet stuff off as soon as possible and dry yourself as best you can.

Wrap up warm. Put on all your warm layers, even if it feels like overkill at the time. Non-insulating fiddly items are often not worth the hassle. Who needs underwear anyway? Prioritise your core (upper half) to start with.

Get moving and warm up slowly. Once you are dressed, walk around, jog on the spot or do a little dance. Anything that gets you moving and helps you start to warm up slowly

1 Post-swim hot drink and contemplation © Jane Sendall   **2** Wonderful wetsuit swimmers at Loch Insh

from the inside. However tempting it is, never go straight from the cold into a hot shower – it can cause sudden cooling of the core, leading to dizziness or even collapse. Wait until you've warmed up again before showering.

Have something to eat and drink. One of the joys of outdoor swimming is huddling around afterwards, sipping hot drinks and sharing something to eat. Our bodies generate heat by metabolising food, so a post-swim snack is pretty much essential. The benefit of the warm drink is primarily psychological, but it still helps. Be mindful that flasks can be very effective at keeping drinks hot – sometimes too hot! Be careful not to scald yourself.

Don't rush off. Don't attempt to drive (or ride a bike) until your core temperature has recovered. Driving and shivering are not a good combination. If your core temperature drops too much and you become hypothermic, it can also affect your cognitive abilities.

Be a good swim pal. Never leave your swim buddy on their own after a swim. Even if someone appears completely fine getting out

of the water, they may be a shivering wreck ten minutes later. If you see someone struggling to get a neoprene sock off or shivering too much to get dressed, help them. Equally, ask for help if you are struggling.

Tidy up and leave no trace. Make sure that you don't leave anything behind and, even better, pick up some litter and leave your swimming spot better than you found it.

It's up to you

Swim at your own risk. Remember, it is up to you to decide whether it is safe to swim at any swimming location on any given day.

For more information on safe swimming, please check out:

- » Outdoor Swimming Society: *www.outdoorswimmingsociety.com*
- » *Outdoor Swimmer* magazine: *www.outdoorswimmer.com*
- » Royal Life Saving Society: *www.rlss.org.uk*
- » Royal National Lifeboat Institution: *www.rnli.org*

Key

 Parking

Public transport

WC Toilets

Swimming spot

X Danger area

1

2

1 Snow swim, Loch Morlich © Bernie McGee

In an emergency
If someone gets into difficulty in the water:

» Call **999** or **112**.
» If you are by the coast or an estuary, ask for the **Coastguard**.
» If you are inland (river or loch with road access), ask for **Fire Service** and **Ambulance**.
» If you are in a mountainous area or far from the nearest road, ask for **Police** and then **Mountain Rescue**.

You will need to provide your exact location (ideally an address, six-figure grid reference or a named location or feature).

Be prepared – no one ever plans to get into difficulty, but you never know when you, someone you are with or a stranger you come across in the water may need emergency assistance. Make sure you are prepared by doing the following.

» Make sure your phone is **fully charged**.
» Download the free **OS Locate** app – this is a fast and highly accurate means of pinpointing your exact location on an OS map. It has an inbuilt GPS system, so you don't need mobile signal, but you will need to switch on your device's location services for this to work.
» Register for the **999 SMS service**. Text the word 'register' to 999 and follow the instructions. You should only use SMS to contact the emergency services if you have no other option, but it is a useful way of getting through in situations where you have low battery or poor signal.

In your SMS outline the rescue service you require, your exact location and the details of the emergency.
www.emergencysms.org.uk

More information:

» *www.rnli.org/safety/respect-the-water*
» *www.rlss.org.uk/how-to-rescue-someone-from-drowning*
» *www.firescotland.gov.uk/your-safety/outdoors/water-safety/what-to-do-if-you-see-someone-in-the-water*

Equipment

WHAT'S IN MY KIT BAG?
The essentials
- » swimming costume (the brighter the better)
- » goggles
- » silicone swimming hat
- » tow float
- » changing towel
- » changing mat
- » dry bag to put wet kit into afterwards
- » flask of hot drink
- » woolly hat for afterwards
- » extra warm layer for afterwards

If it is cold
- » neoprene gloves and socks
- » extra silicone swimming hat (I often wear two) and/or a woolly hat (for swimming in)
- » earplugs
- » even more extra warm stuff for afterwards
- » thermometer

Sometimes I add
- » swimming shoes (if it is rocky)
- » wetsuit (if I'm coaching)
- » waterproof camera
- » waterproof mobile phone case
- » anti-misting goggle spray

One of the joys of outdoor swimming is that you don't need much equipment to get started, especially if you are just planning to dip. However, once we factor in the chilly Scottish water temperatures, staying in the water for longer and the need to be visible to other water users, choosing the right kit can help to make your swim safer and more enjoyable.

While I choose the 'skins' (non-wetsuit) approach, some may choose to dress in head-to-toe neoprene. Each swimmer is an individual, and it is important to determine what will work best for you. We all swim for different reasons, so we have different needs around kit. If it helps you get into and enjoy the water, then it is the right option for you.

WETSUITS AND SWIMSUITS
I swim in just a swimsuit, mainly because that is what I have always done. I love the feeling of freedom it gives me in the water and the tingle of cold water on my skin.

Despite my aversion to wearing one, I actually do think wetsuits are wonderful. They keep you warm, help you stay in the water for longer and their added buoyancy helps you to float, which means you will have to put less effort in to keep your head above water if you get tired. They can also make you a bit faster too.

General watersports and shortie wetsuits are absolutely fine for getting started. If you want to continue dunking and dipping, or if you swim mainly breaststroke, you might want to stick with one of these suits rather than splashing out on anything more technical. They are not as flexible as swim-specific wetsuits but tend to be available in a larger range of sizes and are pretty affordable. Separate neoprene shorts, leggings and tops are also an option.

Swim-specific wetsuits are a bigger investment and generally cost upwards of £100. A fully made-to-measure suit can cost over £500. Many suits are designed for triathletes and front-crawl swimmers, but you can get neutral buoyancy suits and some specifically for breaststroke. They need to be very tight fitting and pulled in tight at the armpit and crotch areas.

If you are particularly worried about the cold, you can get a thermal wetsuit, or you can wear a rash vest or extra neoprene vest underneath your standard wetsuit.

SWIMMING HAT

A brightly coloured swimming hat is essential to make you visible in the water. It will also help keep your hair dry and your head warm. Super-bright neon colours are the best.

Standard swimming hats are silicone, and you can wear more than one if you want. Another option is a neoprene swimming hat; I advise wearing a brightly coloured silicone hat over the top if it is black.

In the winter, you might want to keep your colourful woolly hat on in the water. I love my winter woolly hat swims but be aware that in some conditions your hat may get soaking wet, so make sure you have a dry one in your bag for afterwards.

GOGGLES

Goggles are useful, even if you intend to swim mostly with your head out of the water. Dipping your eyes under the surface occasionally helps you to see what you are swimming over. The type and style come down to personal preference and face shape. I have a narrow face, so I need narrow-fitting goggles. The most important thing is that they fit you properly and don't leak.

Open-water goggles generally have a wider field of vision than goggles designed to be used in a swimming pool. They also come with various lens options designed to cope with weather conditions – clear, tinted or polarised. If you wear glasses, you can get prescription goggles.

In the colder months, I prefer the larger, mask-type goggles as they cover more of my face and help to minimise brain freeze when I put my face in the water.

TOW FLOATS AND DRY BAGS

A tow float is a brightly coloured waterproof bag filled with air and attached to your waist via a leash and belt. They are an essential piece of kit which will make you a lot more visible in the water – to other swimmers, other water users or whoever is keeping an eye on you from the shore.

There are many sizes and types available, from simple 'bubble' floats (with no internal bag) to waterproof dry bags that you can transport your kit in. The latter can be handy for keeping your valuables inside while you swim (I would always use a waterproof mobile phone case and put valuables, including car keys, inside another small watertight container or bag inside the tow float), or to transport your clothes, shoes, towel and snacks if you want to swim from one point to another.

Although they are a wonderful piece of safety kit, tow floats can sometimes encourage people to swim out beyond their capabilities and lull some swimmers into a false sense of security. Always be aware of your surroundings and know your limits. A tow float is not a substitute for ability, and not all water users will be looking out for swimmers in the water, however brightly coloured you are.

GLOVES AND SOCKS

When we get into cold water, our extremities are likely to feel very cold, very fast. Sometimes the pain in your hands and feet is enough to put you off swimming completely. Neoprene gloves and socks can make a big difference, helping to keep your fingers and toes warm while still allowing the rest of your body to experience that cold water buzz. Socks also offer your feet some protection from stony or squelchy entries.

There are various thicknesses. I tend to wear three-millimetre gloves and socks when it is chilly and five-millimetre when it is really cold. It is important that they are tight fitting – if in doubt, try a smaller size. Wrist and ankle straps can also help stop them from filling up with water.

1 Keeping dry in a waterproof robe (umbrella optional!) **2** Slip-on/off swim shoes for before and after swimming
3 Brightly coloured hats, bright tow floats and beaming smiles **4** Colourful SwimWild hats

SWIMMING SHOES

Sometimes you need something more substantial than a neoprene sock to protect your feet from rocky entries or exits or submerged debris in the water.

I once cut my foot on a submerged glass bottle. Thankfully, I was wearing thick neoprene socks and the cut wasn't too deep. If I hadn't been wearing swimming socks, it would have needed stitches; in hindsight, I should have worn swimming shoes or boots with a thicker sole.

Slip-on neoprene aqua shoes with a grippy sole (such as those used for paddleboarding or general watersports) are suitable for this, as are plastic jelly shoes. Wetsuit boots are also useful, but I find them challenging to swim in.

If you don't want to wear shoes in the water, wearing a pair of easy-to-slip-off shoes (such as sliders) down to the water's edge can protect your feet until you get into the water.

EARPLUGS

Many people wear earplugs while swimming to prevent water from getting trapped in their ears, which can cause dizziness and vertigo and lead to infections.

I always wear earplugs in cold water to protect against surfer's ear – a condition in which the ear canal develops bony growths which can only be fixed by surgery.

There are many types and styles. I use silicone putty earplugs as they are the only ones I can get to stay in my ears.

TOWELS AND CHANGING ROBES

Don't forget your towel! As outdoor swimmers, we end up getting changed in car parks or by the water's edge. Getting dressed becomes a bit of an art. Having a large changing towel or robe makes the process a lot easier.

My original changing robe was two bath towels sewed together, and other swimmers often wore dressing gowns down to the beach.

xix

There are many purpose-designed towelling robes available these days, and I change under a hooded, knee-length poncho towel. I use mine every time I swim and, at around £20–£60, I would say it's a great investment.

Then we come on to the ubiquitous oversized waterproof insulated sports cloaks that seem to be the 'uniform' of outdoor swimmers. They are great for keeping you dry, sheltered from the wind and, most importantly, warm. Are they worth the high (often £150 or more) price tag? Well, I suppose it depends on how much you use it. I practically live in mine, and it has lasted for over five years (and is still going strong), so I would say yes. It is like stepping into a warm hug after a swim. But you certainly don't need one – a poncho towel is much more useful.

CHANGING MAT
Having something to stand on insulates you from the cold ground and helps keep you off the mud or sand while you are changing. I use a section of an old foam yoga mat, but I've seen other people use bathmats or kids' play mats.

AFTER-SWIM KIT
You may have noticed that many of the items in my kit bag are for after my swim. Having the right kit to help you get warm afterwards is more important than what kit you choose to wear in the water. Even on relatively warm days, I ensure I have a hot drink, a woolly hat and extra warm layers in my bag, even if I don't end up using them.

Lots of loose-fitting layers are best for helping you warm up after a swim. Have you ever tried putting on a pair of jeans or tight leggings after a cold swim when you are starting to get the shivers? Believe me, it is not easy and will take you a lot longer than pulling on a pair of baggy tracksuit bottoms.

Never underestimate the number of layers you can put on when you get out of the water. In the winter, I have been known to wear multiple base layers, three fleeces (with hoods), two woolly hats, two down jackets (with hoods) and a big warm robe over the top. Thick socks and gloves (or mittens that can be easier to put on if you are really cold) are also essential in the colder months.

KIT BAG
Finally, you'll need something to carry all this stuff in.

There is no need to invest in anything fancy to carry your kit – a large bag-for-life or plastic garden trug (flexible bucket with handles) will do the job nicely if you don't need to carry your kit too far. In the colder months, an insulated shopping bag can be handy. Place a hot water bottle inside it, and everything inside will be toasty warm after your swim.

Don't forget you'll also need a dry bag to separate your soggy kit from your dry kit after your swim.

There are, of course, special swim-specific kit bags that you can buy if you want to. My everyday swimming bag is a large (45-litre) roll-top dry bag with rucksack straps. For swims with a longer walk, I use my normal walking rucksack with my swim kit in a dry bag inside.

1 Diving down into the depths © Sian Jenkins/Susanne Masters **2** The view from beneath © Susanne Masters

Safety – freshwater lochs

Before moving to the Highlands, I did almost all my swimming in the sea. Now I'm an absolute freshwater convert! Living in the Cairngorms National Park, I am lucky to be surrounded by many beautiful lochs and rivers, and I love the feeling of the fresh, silky-smooth water on my skin. While there are no tides to worry about, there are a few other things to consider when taking a freshwater dip.

WATER TEMPERATURE

Smaller lochs have a greater temperature range than large lochs, some warming up to around 20 °C in the summer and some plunging down to 0 °C and freezing over in the winter. Sunshine warms them quickly, but rainfall, especially with spring snowmelt, can cause the temperature to plummet by several degrees in a very short space of time, meaning the water can feel very different from one day to the next.

Larger lochs act more like the sea, taking longer to warm and cool, with less extreme water temperatures across the year. Deep lochs are very unlikely to freeze; however, that also means that they are less likely to be particularly warm in the summer months. For example, after several years of regular swimming in Loch Ness, I noticed that the temperature rarely dipped below 5 °C in the winter and was often still around the 10–12 °C mark in the middle of summer. Brrr!

BE AWARE OF THE WIND

Do not underestimate the power of the wind to blow you off course, tangle you in your tow float leash or create waves that slap you in the face. Long lochs can also have surprisingly big waves as the wind funnels between the hills.

Stick closer to the shore, try to make yourself as streamlined as possible to cut through the waves, clip your tow float directly to your belt (getting rid of the leash) and learn to enjoy those splashy swims. Remember that the added wind chill will also be cooling you down more quickly.

DEEP, DARK WATER

One of the first things I noticed when I started swimming in my local lochs was how dark the water was. It can be quite disconcerting if you are used to swimming in the sea. It certainly took me a while to get used to the black, peaty water (not helped by my overactive imagination and legends of monsters lurking in the depths).

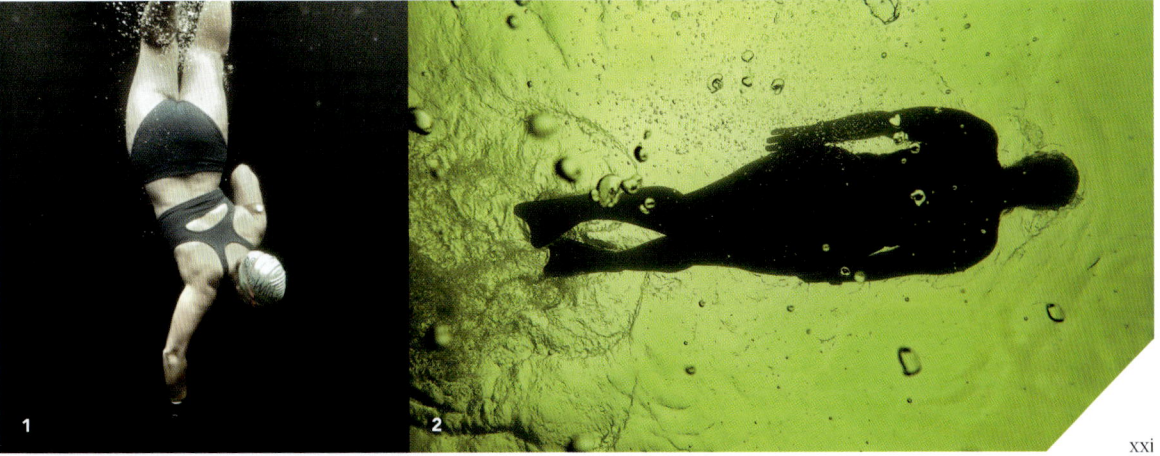

1   2

A decade on, and I still get the occasional heebie-jeebies, but if Nessie or one of her friends hasn't eaten me yet, they are obviously not interested in swimmers!

Watch out for shelving entries and steep drop-offs. One moment you can be paddling happily in shallow water, then suddenly, the bottom disappears, and you can find yourself in deep, dark water, which can feel very different, especially if you are not used to it. If you do find yourself starting to panic, hold on to your tow float, or float on your back with your arms outstretched (like a star), and take several slow, deep breaths.

BIOSECURITY

As swimmers, we don't want to be responsible for transferring invasive and harmful species and bacteria between swimming locations. Ensure that you **check**, **clean** and **dry** all of your kit after each swim to make sure there are no alien species dangling off your costume, wrapped around your goggle straps or stuck to your neoprene shoes. If you are planning to swim in more than one location on the same day, then make sure you have different kit for each swim.

WATER QUALITY

We are blessed with some beautifully clean freshwater swimming options. Very few inland waterways are currently tested for water quality by the Scottish Environment Protection Agency (SEPA), but watersports centres may undertake their own regular testing. Here are a few factors to take into consideration so you can make your own assessment.

You need to be particularly careful during and after periods of high rainfall as this can cause or increase levels of pollution in the water due to sewage overflows or increased runoff from farmland (waste or chemicals). You also need to take care when water levels are unusually low, as less water flow means pollutants can become more concentrated in a particular area, not diluting and dispersing in the same way as they normally would.

Blue–green algae

Blue–green algae is something to look out for in the summer, particularly around the edges of smaller, shallower lochs. It occurs during long periods of warm weather and calm conditions and looks like a layer of greenish scum on the water surface. This algae can be poisonous to dogs and toxic to humans. It is more likely to cause a skin or eye irritation but, in more severe cases, it can cause vomiting and other side effects.

Be aware of local signage and check out the SEPA-endorsed **Bloomin' Algae** app, which helps identify algal blooms, as well as tracking and recording where they are happening.

Swimmer's itch and duck fleas

If you ever get out of the loch and find yourself covered in bites, it is likely to be what is known as swimmer's itch, caused by 'duck fleas'. These are not actually fleas but larvae of a duck parasite that is transmitted via duck poo – delightful!

Thankfully, these are only really a problem when the water is really warm (reports suggest they prefer water of 20 °C and above – not temperatures we often get in Scotland), but the itch can be horrible and last for days, so it's best to avoid the shallows where ducks are and swim further out where the water is cooler. When you get out of the water, dry yourself vigorously with a towel and shower (in cool or lukewarm water) as soon as possible.

Weil's disease

Weil's disease is a rare bacterial infection, most likely to be picked up when entering or exiting stagnant water or after heavy rains. Cuts and abrasions can get infected when they come into contact with water containing contaminated soil and/or urine of wild or farm animals. Another reason to protect your feet (and hands) when entering the water.

1 Crystal-clear river water   **2** Shahjahan getting ready for a river swoosh

Safety – rivers & waterfalls

Rivers and waterfalls are a great reminder of the immense power of water to shape the landscape. Upland river catchments respond rapidly to rainfall, leading to high flow rates at peak times. Tranquil rivers and trickling waterfalls can quickly turn into raging torrents and powerful cascades with deadly undercurrents. Whatever the character of a river, when the flow is high it presents a range of significant dangers to swimmers.

RIVER LEVELS

Never swim if a river is high and fast flowing, flooded or in spate. If you are exploring a new river swimming spot, make sure you do so when water levels are low. You can find useful historical and up-to-date river level data on the SEPA website: *www2.sepa.org.uk/waterlevels*

For river locations in this book, I have provided links to the SEPA data where possible. As a rule, if the flow looks a bit too fast or you are unsure, **do not swim**.

ASSESS THE FLOW AND CHECK FOR HAZARDS

Always make your own assessment of a river before entering the water. Observe the river from the side and above (if possible). Identify where the water is particularly shallow or deep and where the current runs fastest – usually in the centre of the river or on the outside of a bend. You can even throw sticks or leaves in to check the speed of the flow.

Look for evidence of submerged objects and unusual flow patterns on the water surface, such as bubbles, foam, white water, swirling eddies and waves. Circulating currents can be dangerous, pinning you in one place, and bubbling white water (such as at the base of a waterfall) is highly aerated, which impacts buoyancy, meaning you are more likely to sink.

MAKE A PLAN

Always make sure you have a good exit plan before you get in. If swimming in a river pool, try to get in and out where the water runs shallow and always swim against the flow first. If swimming from point to point, thoroughly check your exit and entry points before you get in.

GETTING IN

Even though you have assessed the water from the side, it is still important to be cautious when entering the water. Protect your feet with neoprene socks or shoes – bashing your ankle or knee on a submerged rock is easy to do.

1

2

Even if the location is familiar, the riverbed may have changed since you last swam there – pop your goggles on and have a good look.

THE COLD

Snowmelt and runoff from the surrounding hills mean that river water can often feel colder than surrounding lochs or the sea. Get in slowly, and *never jump straight in* without acclimatising first.

Some river and waterfall swimming spots can feel like adventure playgrounds, with lots of places to explore, rocks to scramble along and swooshes to enjoy. Try not to get carried away, as it is easy to stay in too long if you get distracted. Keep your swims short, and make sure you have lots of warm layers to put on afterwards.

JUMPING AND DIVING

If you want to jump or dive in, it is essential to get into the water first and carefully test the depth of the area to ensure it is completely clear of hazards. Never assume that because somewhere is known as a local diving spot that it will be safe on the day you decide to go. There may not be sufficient depth, or obstacles (such as rocks or branches) may have moved into what was previously a safe entry spot.

THE WEIGHT OF WATER

Do not swim directly beneath the cascade of a waterfall. If you do, you may be placing yourself under a weight of water which is powerful and dangerous.

The power of the water varies with the flow rate, and the height of a waterfall affects its strength. Below the surface, multi-directional circulating currents mean that you can get trapped below the surface. Keep your distance and admire the waterfall from the edge of the pool.

Safety – sea swimming

Sea swimming can be an absolute joy; however, the ever-changing nature of coastal environments means that a swimming location you may consider perfectly 'safe' one day may be completely unswimmable the next. The presence of tides and currents make sea swimming an inherently risky activity. It's essential to have at least a basic understanding of tides and currents, along with other marine hazards, if you plan to swim in the sea.

WATER TEMPERATURE

Sea temperatures are more stable than those of inland waters, taking longer to rise and fall. The sea around Scotland is at its coldest around February or March (5–7 °C and at its warmest around August (14–17 °C). Spring water temperatures can easily catch people out – even if there is a heatwave in April, the sea temperature may still only be around 8 °C, only reaching above 10 °C in May. In contrast, autumn temperatures can be surprisingly pleasant, hovering around 12–14 °C in October.

For more localised information on current and historical sea temperatures, see *www.seatemperature.info*

TIDES

In very basic terms, tides are the vertical rise and fall of the levels of the ocean caused by the gravitational interaction between the earth, the moon and the sun. *Spring tides* have the largest tidal range (highest high tides and lowest low tides) and occur twice per lunar month when the sun, earth and moon are in a direct line. *Neap tides* have a smaller tidal range and occur when the sun and moon are at right angles to each other.

1 Diving into the crystal-clear water © Becca Harvey   **2** Big splash © Becca Harvey   **3** Summer sea dip © Becca Harvey

The level of the tide can vastly affect the appearance and character of a beach, impacting access to the water. Some beaches may be very stony at high tide but perfectly sandy at low tide, while others may only be swimmable at high tide. When swimming at a new location, it is always best to check the beach at low tide to identify any rocks or hazards that may become submerged as the tide rises.

TIDAL CURRENT AND FLOW

The tide will not push you towards or drag you away from the shore with any noticeable effect (apart from in areas with exceptionally high tidal ranges). Instead, the tide flows sideways along the beach. As you enter, the water currents will either be racing to the left, to the right or not at all. The tide changes direction roughly every six hours, with more water moving during the middle two hours of both an incoming (*flood*) and outgoing (*ebb*) tide, resulting in much stronger sideways currents during these times.

Slack water occurs around one hour on either side of high or low tide, where there is very little movement in either direction. This is generally the safest time to swim; the absence of a flow means that less effort is required to swim and there is less likelihood of drifting away from your entry point on the shore.

On spring tides, more water is moving further between the extreme high and low tides. Sideways currents are, therefore, stronger on spring tides than on neap tides.

When planning to swim parallel to the shore, take a moment to work out which way the tide is flowing (if at all). Assuming you plan to start and finish in the same place, always swim in the most difficult direction first (i.e. against the tide), so that you will have an easier swim on your way back. This is really important, as if you do it the other way round, you can end up going much further than you planned as it feels easy, but then have to battle back to the start and get too cold or tired in the process.

WIND AGAINST TIDE

Cross-shore winds can either assist your progress or make for uncomfortable swimming conditions. When the wind is blowing in the same direction as the tidal flow, the sea will be smoother, and it is easy to cruise downstream. If the wind and tide are travelling in opposing directions, the sea can get very choppy, slapping you in the face and making it generally unpleasant for swimming.

WAVES

Playing in the waves can be wonderful, but waves can also catch you out, knock you over

or send you tumbling. Waves tend to come in 'sets' of several larger waves interspersed with smaller waves. Occasionally, a set of unexpectedly large waves might come through. Always keep an eye out, and don't turn your back on the sea.

There are three main types of waves.

Spilling waves: gentle waves where the top of the wave gradually tumbles down the face of the wave. These are usually found on gently sloping or flat beaches and are generally safe for swimmers, as long as you are careful.

Plunging or dumping waves: powerful waves that break with tremendous force. These occur on more steeply sloping beaches and are dangerous as they have the force to knock you off your feet.

Surging waves: a wall of water that may never break. These are most likely around rocky areas and shorelines with very steep profiles. They travel at high speeds and can be incredibly dangerous due to their strong backwash (pulling or sucking effect).

The height of the tide can also affect how waves break along the shore. For example, at some beaches spilling waves occur at low tide but, as the tide rises and waves hit a steeper part of the beach, they will become more dangerous, despite the swell being exactly the same. The wave heights will be the same, but their shape and speed of breaking will be completely different.

RIP CURRENTS

A rip current is a narrow channel of water flowing back out to sea. They can be dangerous to swimmers as they can sweep people out into deep water very quickly.

Rips can occur on any beaches at any time (including at slack tide) as long as there are breaking waves (white water). The bigger the waves, the larger the rip is likely to be. Rips can also form where river estuaries run into the sea.

Identifying a rip current

» **Absence of breaking waves.** Look out for a calm channel between areas of white water – like a river flowing out to sea. The calm gap in the waves can be deceptive as it might look like a good place to get into the water to avoid the waves. It is actually the most dangerous place to get in.

» **Discoloured water and floating debris.** The discolouration is created by the current picking up sand in the water as it moves out to sea.

» **Headlands and artificial structures.** Rip currents are also common in areas with piers, jetties and anything else that sticks out from the beach.

How to escape a rip current

» **Stay calm** and resist the urge to swim directly back to shore against the current. If you fight the rip, you will become exhausted.

» If you can stand, **wade** rather than swim.

» **Try to move sideways**, parallel to the shore, until you are clear of the channel and then swim back to shore.

» If you can't wade or swim out of the rip, **remain floating** until the rip weakens, then swim back to shore or continue signalling for help.

» If you are struggling, remember to **keep calm, face the shore and signal for help**.

For more information, see *www.rnli.org/safety/know-the-risks/rip-currents*

WILDLIFE

The coast of Scotland is rich in wildlife. I love looking out for starfish or crabs scuttling across the sand and am often joined on my swims by curious seals. If you want to find out more about the wildlife you may encounter while swimming, it is worth getting hold of a copy of *Wild Waters*, written by scientist and swimmer Susanne Masters (and illustrated by me).

Here are a few things to think about if you encounter marine wildlife in the water or on the beach.

- » **Be aware:** keep a lookout in the water for nearby wildlife and keep an eye on their movements.
- » **Keep your distance:** never deliberately approach marine wildlife or swim straight towards it.
- » **Keep calm:** don't splash or scream. Keep movements steady and predictable.
- » **Be flexible:** be prepared to change your swim route to minimise disturbance. Always allow an escape route for the animal.
- » **Tread lightly:** be careful of where you put your feet. Some species are vulnerable to physical damage.

Never approach mothers with young, or young seal pups alone on the beach. It is quite common for seal pups to be left for short periods of time. They are not normally stranded, just waiting for their mothers to return. Adult female seals are shy and unlikely to rejoin a pup if there is activity nearby. If you find a stranded marine mammal, call the British Divers Marine Life Rescue hotline (T: **01825 765 546** (24-hour)) or Scottish SPCA Animal Helpline (T: **03000 999 999**). For more information, see *www.bdmlr.org.uk*

JELLYFISH

Jellyfish can be less welcome companions in the water during your swims in the summer months. Some of them are completely harmless (such as the moon jellyfish), but some can give you a nasty sting. The most common stingers you may come across are lion's mane jellyfish and compass jellyfish.

While head-butting a lion's mane is not advisable (yes, I have accidentally done this), the thought of a jellyfish sting is often worse than the sting itself. Generally, it feels like a bad nettle sting, which gradually eases. Of course, some stings can be worse than others, and you need to be particularly careful if you might

have an allergic reaction to one. One way to avoid getting stung is to put on a wetsuit, long-sleeved costume or rash vest when swimming during jellyfish season. Larger, mask-type goggles can also help to protect your face.

If you do get stung, stay in the water if you can. Salt water helps to ease the sting, and you may find it has almost disappeared by the time you get out. If it is still painful, rinse the sting under hot water (if possible), take an antihistamine and apply zinc cream (such as Sudocrem) to the area to ease the sting. If it is really painful and does not ease quickly, consider going to a minor injuries unit.

FORECASTS AND PLANNING

- » Always check **tide times** when planning your swim. Is it a neap or spring tide? What phase will the tide be in when you plan to swim (high or low slack water; ebb or flow)? *www.tidetimes.org.uk* *www.willyweather.co.uk*
- » Check the **weather and wind forecast** before you swim. Take note of wind direction, strength, wave and swell height. I always check multiple sites. *www.metoffice.gov.uk* (general weather forecast) *www.windfinder.com* (wind forecast – includes wave height) *www.magicseaweed.com* (surf forecast – handy for the areas it covers)
- » Check **water quality**, especially if it has been raining, as sewerage discharges into the sea are more likely. *www2.sepa.org.uk/bathingwaters* (SEPA bathing water testing – seasonal water quality information for over 80 sites around Scotland)
- » **Safer Seas & Rivers Service** app (data also available at *www.sas.org.uk/map*)

Always be prepared to change your plans according to the conditions on the day. Most importantly, **if in doubt – do not swim!**

ARGYLL
& THE ISLES

Previous page Sorobaidh Bay, Tiree **Opposite** Isle of Coll

1 The Blue Pool, Glen Rosa © Emma Norton
2 Mini waterfalls running down the valley of Glen Rosa © Shutterstock/Richard Bowden

Glen Rosa, Arran

Arran's miniature version of Skye's Fairy Pools, Glen Rosa has a couple of small sections of river deep enough to swim in.

The Blue Pool is a tiny plunge pool beneath a wee waterfall on Glenrosa Water. It's a beautiful place to dip, with spectacular views up the glen towards Goatfell, Arran's highest mountain. On blue-sky days, the water really does look incredibly blue. If you get the spot to yourself, it's a little slice of river pool paradise.

Further downstream is another lovely little pool beneath a wooden bridge which isn't as deep as the Blue Pool but is still large enough for a dip.

THE SWIM

At first sight, the Blue Pool can be a little underwhelming as it really is very small. Having said that, it is actually bigger and deeper than it looks when you first approach it from the path. I've always spent a long time playing about in the Blue Pool, marvelling at the water clarity and soaking up the views.

Getting in is a case of stepping down or sliding off the rocks, so you must commit yourself to taking the plunge. I've always found the water here surprisingly cold, even in August. Make sure you have some warm clothes to wear afterwards, even if it's a warm day. Getting out, there is an underwater ledge that you can use as a step.

Downstream, the Bridge Pool is a bit more tucked away and another fabulous place for a refreshing dip. It is also small, and the entry is just a couple of steps down from the grassy bank on the far side.

TECHNICAL INFORMATION

DESCRIPTION **river pool**   RIVER **Glenrosa Water**   ELEVATION (BRIDGE POOL) **50m**   ELEVATION (BLUE POOL) **60m**   ACCESS **2.5km walk, mainly on a good track**   ENTRY **step down or slide into the water from the rocks**   GOOD FOR **quick dips; amazing views; crystal-clear water**   LOCAL GROUP **Arran Open Water Swimmers**   LOCATION **55.6011, -5.2036**

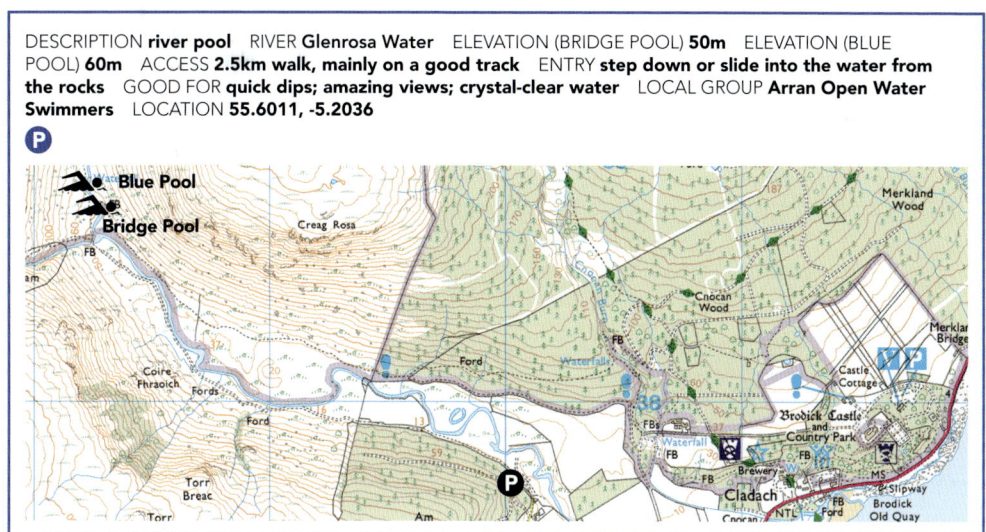

Getting there

From Brodick take the B880 towards Blackwaterfoot and take the first right turn signposted *Cart Track, Glen Rosa*. Follow the single-track road for around one kilometre until you get to Glen Rosa Campsite. Around 100 metres past the gate, there is a small car park. There are no facilities.

You'll need to get there early (or late) in the summer to get a parking place.

Access

Follow the main gravel track up the glen. After just over two kilometres you will reach a wooden bridge with a waterfall on your left. Cross the bridge and continue along the path, which has some rough sections.

For the Bridge Pool, take the small track on the right after around 100 metres. It takes you to a smaller wooden bridge with a pool on the downstream side.

For the Blue Pool, stick on the main track that follows the stream up the valley for a further 150 metres. The pool is on the right, just beneath a small waterfall, soon after the track returns to being close to the river. Downstream of the pool is a huge flat rock that nearly spans the whole width of the river; upstream there is a distinctive large boulder.

Refreshments

» **Janie's**, Cladach. Great little cafe with delicious coffee, lovely home-made cakes and a shop selling freshly roasted coffee. Just a couple of doors along is the **Arran Cheese Shop**, which is worth a look if you like cheese!

» **The Wineport**, Cladach. Bar and bistro with a large beer garden. A good place for lunch or just coffee and cake.

» **Little Rock**, Brodick. Amazing cafe behind a crazy golf course. Very busy and popular but when you taste the food you'll understand why! Great for breakfast, coffee or lunch.

Carradale, Kintyre

The Kintyre peninsula is well known due to Sir Paul McCartney and Denny Laine's iconic song, 'Mull of Kintyre'. Off the beaten track, it isn't a place you pass through on your way to somewhere else; you really only go there if it is your destination. While the west coast can be wild and unpredictable, the sheltered eastern side of the peninsula is a haven for swimmers.

The village of Carradale lies a little over halfway down the east coast of Kintyre, and has two exceptional swimming beaches.

CARRADALE BAY
Protected to the east by the rocky headland of Carradale Point, this lengthy sandy beach is a lovely place for longer swims parallel with the shore. The beach is nearly one kilometre in length from end to end, and if you catch it on a calm, sunny day, it is hard to resist a dip in the sparkling water.

I prefer swimming here at high tide. The beach stays shallow for quite a long way out, so you can easily swim within your depth.

PORT RIGH
Small but perfectly formed, this little bay is my favourite place to swim on the Kintyre peninsula. It's a very sheltered semi-circular bay with fantastic views across the Kilbrannan Sound towards the Isle of Arran.

The entry is sandy, with some pebbles and stones. The bay is only around 100 metres across, but a perfect place for peaceful dips. The water clarity has always been excellent when I've swum here, revealing a fascinating underwater world.

TECHNICAL INFORMATION

Carradale Bay
DESCRIPTION **beach** ORIENTATION **south** TIDES **best at high tide** ACCESS **parking by the beach** ENTRY **sand** GOOD FOR **longer swims; wildlife spotting; playing in the waves** LOCATION **55.5813, -5.4731**

Port Righ
DESCRIPTION **beach** ORIENTATION **east** TIDES **best at high tide** ACCESS **1.2km walk from car park; steps down from the road** ENTRY **sand; gravel in places** GOOD FOR **short swims; beautiful views; sunrise swims** LOCATION **55.5854, -5.4646**

Getting there – Carradale

Take the B879 towards Carradale. Turn right after Carradale Primary School, signposted *Port Righ* and *Carradale Bay parking*. After 300 metres (where the road bends to the left) there is a gate straight ahead. Go through the gate (make sure you close it behind you) and continue along the track. There is a second gate before you reach the grassy car park. I've found that this is the best place to park for both beaches.

Access – Carradale Bay

Walk down the sandy path to the beach.

Access – Port Righ

Walk back along the track from the car park and then follow the lane and walk down the steps to the beach (1.2 kilometres). There is also very limited parking on the lane directly above Port Righ – please don't park at the end of the road as this is a turning area.

Refreshments

» **Blackbird Tearoom**, Carradale. Brilliant little cafe with delicious home bakes and great coffee.
» **The Glen Bar & Restaurant**, Carradale. Cosy restaurant with a wood-burning stove.
» **Beinn an Tuirc Distillery Cafe**, Torrisdale Castle Estate. Great cafe for post-swim coffee, cakes, lunch or something a bit stronger! Everything is local, fresh and delicious. Indoor and covered outdoor seating. For something a bit special, you can pre-book an afternoon tea.

1

Twin Beaches, Isle of Gigha

Gigha is a wee island paradise. It's the most southerly Inner Hebridean island, yet surprisingly is not as well known as its larger neighbours, which include Islay and Jura. Located just three kilometres off the Kintyre coast, Gigha is easily reached via a 20-minute ferry journey from Tayinloan.

Towards the north of the island, Gigha's Twin Beaches sit on either side of a tombolo, a thin strip of land which connects the main island from the tiny outcrop of Eilean Garbh. Of course, I can never resist swimming on both sides!

THE SWIM

The south-facing beach, Bàgh Rubha Ruaidh, is best at high tide. It is pretty flat and takes a while to get deep enough to swim. I love snorkelling in the shallows and looking at the different kinds of seaweed in the bay.

The north-facing beach, Bàgh na Dòirlinne, is truly stunning, with white sand and turquoise water, and is generally better for swimming.

The entry is gradually sloping and it gets deep enough to swim more quickly than the south-facing beach. It is around 150 metres across the bay, and I love swimming widths and practising handstands on this side.

Be aware that small boats occasionally anchor in this sheltered bay.

TECHNICAL INFORMATION

DESCRIPTION **beach** ORIENTATION **south and north** TIDES **both best at high tide** ACCESS **500m walk or cycle from ferry to beaches** ENTRY **sand** GOOD FOR **double dipping; turquoise water; wildlife watching** LOCATION **55.7229, -5.7346**

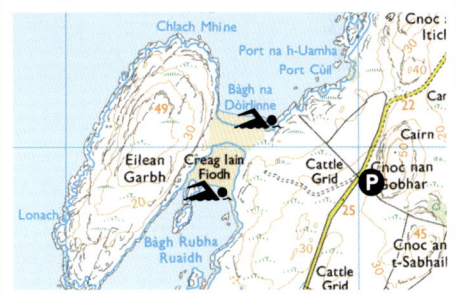

Getting there

The ferry to the Isle of Gigha runs from Tayinloan (where there is a car park available if you don't want to take your car with you). It is a turn-up-and-go ferry service, with no booking necessary.

Gigha is a small island with only one road and is easy to explore on a bike or on foot. You can hire bikes at Gigha Boats and Activity Centre, which is just as you come off the ferry. The road is reasonably flat and virtually traffic free, so it's ideal for a gentle six-kilometre cycle to the beaches.

From Ardminish, follow the road north until you reach a wooden signpost pointing the way towards the *Twin Beaches*. There is a small amount of parking next to the road.

There are no facilities up at this end of the island.

Access

From the road, head through the gate and follow the (often muddy) track through a grassy field. The track swings to the right; continue straight ahead here down to the beaches.

Refreshments

» **The Nook**, Ardminish. Fresh, local fish and seafood takeaway. Simple and delicious. Seasonal.
» **Ardminish Stores**, Ardminish. Local shop and post office with lots of delicious local supplies, including ice creams from Gigha's Wee Isle Dairy.
» **The Boathouse**, Ardminish. Exceptional seafood restaurant – not cheap but worth every penny! Seasonal.

Ardtalla Beach, Islay

Islay has many beautiful beaches, but the waves and currents on the wild Atlantic west coast can be treacherous. Do not try entering the water at Machir Bay (Kilchoman), Saligo Bay or Lossit Bay, as they have strong currents and dangerous rips.

There are a number of incredible swimming options around other parts of the coast. My favourite is Ardtalla Beach (Tràigh Bhàn) on the east coast. Protected by a series of skerries and rocks, it is superbly sheltered from almost all wind directions, resulting in a shallow (but deep enough to swim), lagoon-like bay with spectacular water clarity.

With white sand, lush vegetation lining the beach and views across to the Kintyre peninsula, it is one of those stunning places that I feel like I never want to leave, especially on a sunny day. I've also been lucky enough to spot sea eagles at the far end of the beach and curious seals watching me as I swim.

THE SWIM

The beach has a lovely, gently sloping entry. You can swim here at any time; however, it is most protected from southerly winds at low tide.

It is an excellent place for shorter swims and snorkelling in the shallows. The lagoon is around 150 metres wide, and I've managed to swim lengths of about 250 metres at high tide. It becomes very shallow at low tide but is still deep enough to paddle and swim closer to the rocks.

Stick within the lagoon and watch out for submerged rocks towards the northern end of the beach.

1 The author at Ardtalla Beach, Islay © Jeremy Hubbard

TECHNICAL INFORMATION

DESCRIPTION **beach**   ORIENTATION **east and
south-east**   TIDES **can swim any time; most
sheltered at low tide**   ACCESS **650m walk to
the beach**   ENTRY **sand**   GOOD FOR **sheltered
swims; seal spotting; shallow water**   LOCAL
GROUP **Islay Salty Souls**   LOCATION **55.7150,
-6.0365**

Getting there
From Port Ellen take the A846 towards the
southern distilleries and follow the road all the
way to the end, passing Laphroaig, Lagavulin,
Ardbeg and the Kildalton Cross. When you

reach Claggain Bay, keep driving to the end of
the bay and park in the small car park on the
right. This is the end of the official road.

There is additional parking on the grass at
Claggain Bay – another lovely beach, particularly at the sandier, southern end of the bay.

Access
From the parking area, go through the gate and
follow the track, which bends to the right. Once
you've passed the first stone wall, head right
across the field. Please be aware that there can
sometimes be cows or sheep grazing here.

Refreshments
» **Ardstream**, Ardbeg Distillery, Ardbeg.
  Fabulous converted airstream trailer by the
  courtyard at Ardbeg Distillery. Serves hot
  and cold drinks, home baking and light
  lunches. Seasonal.
» **SeaSalt Bistro & Takeaway**, Port Ellen.
  Tasty food and good pizzas.
» **The Wee Box**, Playing Fields, Port Ellen.
  Cute little converted horse trailer serving
  delicious hot drinks, home bakes and
  sandwiches. Seasonal.

Easdale Slate Quarries

Easdale is the smallest permanently inhabited island of the Inner Hebrides. For almost three centuries, it was at the centre of the Scottish slate industry; at its peak the island had seven quarries and a community of more than 500 miners.

In 1881 a huge storm seriously flooded and damaged the island's working quarries to such an extent that the industry never properly recovered, although large-scale quarrying continued until the early twentieth century. Easdale is now home to around 60 people, and the quarries have all been flooded.

There are five enclosed quarry 'pools' and a couple that are still open to the sea. I have swum in all of them and can report that some are better for swimming than others. All have stunningly clear blue water and are very deep. They are gloriously sheltered places to swim and lovely and calm even when the sea around the island is rough.

THE SWIM

Although it is possible to swim in all of the pools, only three have suitable entries. The two pools towards the north-west of the island are the easiest to access, and the pool near the south-west point has the best views. All these have sloping slate shingle beaches.

The smallest, L-shaped pool is the most popular for swimming. It is the shallowest and has the most gradually sloping entry. You can stick close to the edge and avoid the deeper sections. Both the other pools get deep very quickly, so be prepared if you don't like deep water.

Be careful, though, as slate can be very sharp. It was so warm last time I visited that I decided not to wear anything on my feet (not a good idea). I managed to get a nasty cut on my toe from carelessly kicking a bit of slate while swimming.

TECHNICAL INFORMATION

DESCRIPTION **flooded quarry**   MAXIMUM DEPTH **90m**   ACCESS **no cars allowed on the island; 750m walk to the first pool**   ENTRY **sloping slate shingle; some pools get deep more quickly than others**   GOOD FOR **sheltered swims; deep water; multiple dips**   LOCATION **56.2930, -5.6619**

Getting there

From the A816 south of Oban, turn on to the B844, signposted *Easdale*. Follow the road over to the Isle of Seil. Once you arrive in Ellenabeich, there is parking close to the jetty and a larger car park around the corner.

There are regular buses from Oban to Ellenabeich, running every day except Sundays.

You don't need to book the ferry to Easdale. There is a little waiting room with a button to call the ferry. The boat is tiny, and there is no undercover area on the boat, so make sure you have wet-weather gear if it is raining. The crossing only takes a few minutes.

1 South-west pool, Easdale, with views across to Mull   **2** High-sided quarry pool, Easdale © Anna Deacon

Access

From the jetty, skirt around the harbour and continue along the path that crosses the northern end of the island. Cross over the narrow section between two pools. At the far end, take a track down to the left, which will take you down to the entry of the high-sided quarry pool.

A little further along the main track, you can follow a small path on the right which will take you down to the entry of the smallest pool.

To get to the third pool, you can continue along the track to the south of the island. The entry for this pool is at the furthest corner so you have to go around the edge (it is a bit rocky at some points) to reach it.

Refreshments

» **The Puffer**, Easdale. The only eating and drinking establishment on the island. Tasty cakes and yummy soup. Seasonal.
» **The Oyster**, Ellenabeich. Great bar and restaurant for before or after your ferry trip over to Easdale. Inside and outside seating.

1 Rocks and sea at Uisken Beach © Jane Sendall   **2** Inlet Beach at Uisken   **3** Uisken Beach © Jeremy Hubbard

Uisken Beach, Mull

Mull's southwestern peninsula, known as the Ross of Mull, has many spectacular beaches and you are spoilt for choice when it comes to swimming. My favourite is Uisken Beach, which has many rocky islands and outcrops and is a popular place to swim, snorkel and paddleboard.

Uisken (*Uisgean* in Gaelic, meaning 'Water-Bay') has views out over the sea to the islands of Colonsay, Jura and Islay. The beach looks quite different depending on the state of the tide. At high tide, the beach is pretty small. At low tide, the bay becomes a lagoon with multiple sheltered options for swimming; you can walk out to some of the small islands too. There is also another little beach tucked into an inlet to the west of the main beach, which is terrific for a dip.

THE SWIM

Swimming here is usually relatively sheltered, especially at low tide when the rocky islands offer more protection. It is pretty shallow and mostly sandy, with some deeper channels. If the wind is blowing in from the south, a channel at the far eastern end of the beach should still be nice and calm. This is only accessible at mid-to-low tide.

The bay is small and fragmented, so this isn't somewhere for longer swims. I love pottering around the bay and exploring the sheltered nooks and crannies of the islands. Remember to wear your goggles, as the underwater landscape is fascinating. There are lots of different types of seaweed with varied textures and colours. I've seen sand eels, flatfish and lots of crabs while I've been swimming.

Watch out for small boats which sometimes anchor in the bay.

TECHNICAL INFORMATION

DESCRIPTION **beach** ORIENTATION **south** TIDES **possible to swim at any time** ACCESS **park right next to the beach; a further 300m walk to inlet** ENTRY **sand** GOOD FOR **crystal-clear water; shorter swims and dips; snorkelling** LOCATION **56.2889, -6.2170**

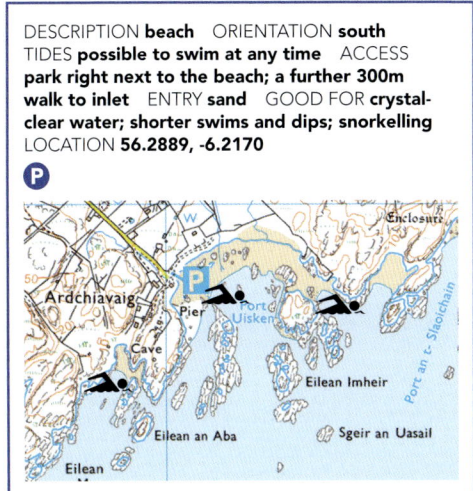

Getting there

Head west on the A849 towards Bunessan. Turn left opposite the car park in Bunessan, sign-posted to the *Police station* and *Toilets*. Take the next left and follow signs to Uisken. As you descend the hill, you get a great view of Arda-lanish Bay on your right. Carry on along the road into *Uisken* and down to the beach, where there is a small parking area not suitable for large vehicles. This can fill up quickly on sunny summer days, but I've always found space at other times.

Access

The car park is right next to the main beach. If you want to walk round to the inlet, follow the little road opposite the car park round to the right; continue as it turns into a track, past a couple of houses and down to the beach.

Refreshments

» **Ardalanish Farm and Isle of Mull Weavers**, Ardalanish. Between April and October, the on-site shop serves hot drinks, ice cream and home-baked pasties.
» **Argyll Arms**, Bunessan. Typical pub grub. Variable opening hours and seasonal.
» If neither of these are open the **Snack Bar** in Fionnphort (inside the ferry terminal) is usually a good bet. It's very basic but you can normally get something hot to eat and drink. Open in line with ferry times.

1 Tràigh an t-Suidhe looking towards Eilean Chalbha © Jeremy Hubbard   **2** Port Ban Beach © Shutterstock/Malago

Iona

Iona is a swimmers' dream, with crystal-clear water and tropical-looking beaches scattered all along its beautiful coastline. I've been lucky enough to visit Iona multiple times over the last few years and have swum in many different locations around the island. I found it impossible to choose just one beach, so here are two of my favourites.

PORT BAN BEACH

Port Ban, whose name comes from the Gaelic for 'White Port', is a pristine white beach of sand made from crushed shells. With cliffs on either side protecting it from the worst of the Atlantic swell, this sheltered inlet is the most popular beach on the island for swimming. It is shallow and sandy with very little chop or current, making it ideal for families and less confident swimmers.

My favourite time to swim is a couple of hours after low tide, as you can swim a reasonable distance while still staying within your depth. Alternatively, you can swim shorter widths of the bay. On an incoming tide, the long, gentle slope releases heat from the sun-warmed sand, making it feel warmer than other beaches around the island. Sunset swims here are spectacular.

TRÀIGH AN T-SUIDHE

I love swimming at Tràigh an t-Suidhe (Strand of the Seat) with its amazing views to Coll, Tiree and the Treshnish Isles – the Dutchman's Cap (easy to spot), Lunga (known for its seabirds) and Fladda (the flat one). On a clear day, you can also see the peaks of Rùm and Skye further in the distance. After my last swim here, I saw a minke whale in the middle of the bay as I was warming up on the shore.

Swimming here is best at high tide. I prefer to head down to the bay's western end and get in close to Eilean Chalbha (Calf Island). This part of the beach tends to be more sheltered than the eastern end, which often has larger waves and stronger currents.

TECHNICAL INFORMATION

Port Ban Beach

DESCRIPTION **beach** ORIENTATION **west**
TIDES **can swim anytime; best a couple of hours
on either side of low tide** ACCESS **2.5km walk
from ferry** ENTRY **sand** GOOD FOR **sheltered
swims; shallow water; sunset dips** LOCATION
56.3328, -6.4276

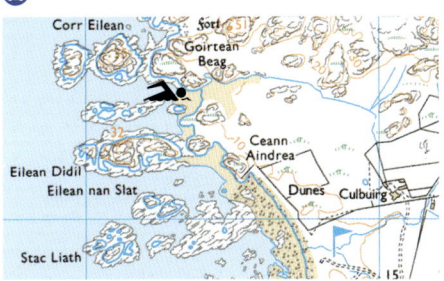

Tràigh an t-Suidhe

DESCRIPTION **beach** ORIENTATION **north**
TIDES **best at high tide** ACCESS **2km walk
from ferry** ENTRY **sand** GOOD FOR
**incredible views; wildlife spotting; turquoise
water** LOCATION **56.3473, -6.3998**

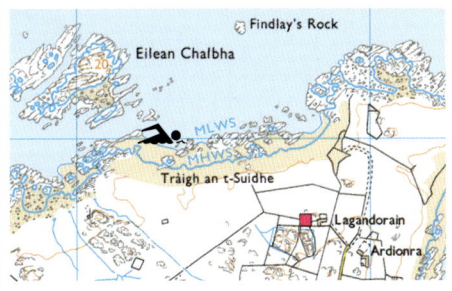

Getting there – Iona

Ferries run to Iona from Fionnphort on Mull,
and it is only a ten-minute journey across the
Sound of Iona. No booking is necessary – just
buy a ticket at the port and go on the next
available sailing.

You have to leave your car parked in
Fionnphort and come across as a foot
passenger as visitors are not allowed to bring
vehicles on to the island. Bicycles are permitted.
There is a regular bus service that runs from
Craignure to Fionnphort.

Once you arrive, you can explore the island
on foot or hire bikes from **Iona Craft Shop**,
which is close to the ferry. The minimum hire
period is three hours.

Access – Port Ban Beach

Port Ban is on the opposite side of the island
to the ferry port. Head south and then west
towards Iona Golf Course. Once you reach the
Bay at the Back of the Ocean, continue north up
the machair before passing through a stile and
a gate. Pass a couple of small coves then Port
Ban Beach is a little further on, down a sandy
track.

Access – Tràigh an t-Suidhe

From the ferry take the road heading north,
past Iona Abbey, to the end of the tarmac. Go
straight ahead through a gate (passing a track
on your left leading to a farm and hostel). Take
the first or second left turn after this to get
down to the beach on the island's northern side.

Refreshments

» **The Rookery Cafe**, Iona Heritage Centre.
Friendly wee cafe with amazing soup and
tasty cakes. Excellent coffee. Seasonal.
» **St Columba Hotel**, Iona. A good place for
lunch or dinner. Inside and outside seating.
Open daily for non-residents.
» **Martyr's Bay**, by the ferry slipway, Iona.
Cafe and bar with great views over the
Sound of Iona to Mull.

Calgary Bay, Mull

My first experience of Calgary Bay was camping by the beach in winter. The wind whistled along the sand, and I got into the sea for a bracing dip, totally falling in love with this beautiful place in the process. I've swum here many times since and have been lucky enough to watch otters fishing near the rocks and eagles soaring overhead.

Calgary Bay is one of the few beaches on Mull backed by sand dunes with fertile grasslands or machair; its name can be traced back to the Gaelic for 'Beach of the Meadow' or 'Pasture'. And yes, the city of Calgary in the province of Alberta in Canada is named after Calgary on Mull. This came about when an officer in the Mounties who was a summer guest of the Calgary House Estate loved the place so much and took the idea back home with him.

THE SWIM

The entry is sandy, and pretty shallow for a fair way out. Be mindful that you can have up to 200 metres extra to walk out across the sand at low tide. This is quite a long way if there is a big wind chill.

You can get in anywhere along the beach and, if conditions allow, it is lovely to swim across the bay, parallel to the shore. It is around 400 metres across the beach (one way).

Be aware that there are some submerged rocks on both sides of the beach and a patch near the middle. If the water is flat and clear, they are easy to spot, but if it is wavy, it is best to stay opposite the path from the car park or at the campsite end.

TECHNICAL INFORMATION

DESCRIPTION **beach**   ORIENTATION **west**
TIDES **possible to swim at any time**   ACCESS
150m walk along track to beach   ENTRY **sand**
GOOD FOR **playing in the waves; swims in the bay; sunset dips**   LOCATION **56.5797, -6.2833**

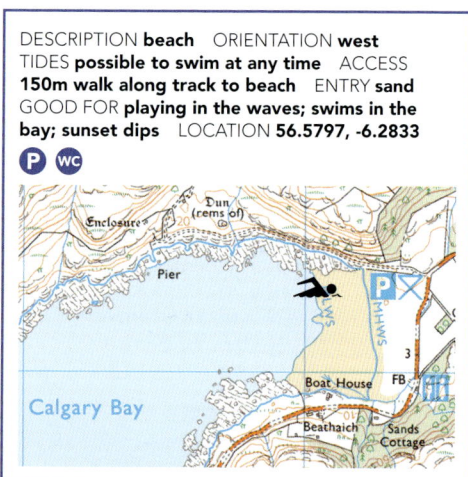

1 Talisker dog enjoying the sand at Calgary Bay   2 Calgary Bay © Walkhighlands
3 First glimpse of Sorobaidh Bay © Alastair Goodridge

Getting there

Head west from Dervaig on the B8073 for about eight kilometres until you reach the beach car park. It is likely to be very busy on sunny days in the summer, so make sure you get there early to get a parking space.

There is an infrequent, weekday bus service from Tobermory to Calgary Bay.

Refreshments

» **Robin's Boat**, Calgary Bay car park. Quirky little takeaway by the beach. Serves ice cream, snacks, sweets and hot drinks. Seasonal. Usually open on sunny days and daily in the school summer holidays.
» **Calgary Farmhouse Cafe**, Calgary. Wonderful cafe at Calgary Arts Centre. Lovely lunch and cakes. Seasonal. Look out near the car park for a beautiful willow selkie and a wooden basking shark sculpture, which are part of the Calgary Art in Nature woodland sculpture trail.

Sorobaidh Bay, Tiree

The beaches of Tiree stretch for miles and miles, and you are spoilt for choice when it comes to places to swim. While the beaches on the west coast are exposed to Atlantic swell and a mecca for lovers of big surf, the south-east-facing shores tend to be much more sheltered and can be great for swimming. The Tiree Polar Bears group regularly meets up at Gott Bay (Silversands), Crossapol Bay and Sorobaidh Bay, and I've been lucky enough to swim with them at all three. I've loved every second of every swim, and each time I visit I really don't want my time on Tiree to end.

Sorobaidh Bay (or Sorby Bay) is my favourite beach for swimming on Tiree – a beautiful 1.4-kilometre stretch of pristine sand with sparkling water and views over towards Mull, Iona and the Treshnish Isles. Protected by the Hynish peninsula to the south-west, the beach is usually sheltered and is a great place for quick dips or longer swims parallel with the shore. Having an excellent cafe just a stone's throw away is an added bonus.

THE SWIM

I prefer swimming here around high tide, but you can swim at any time if you stick close to the shore. You can get in anywhere along the beach, and it is always fairly shallow for quite a long way out.

Be aware that there are some submerged rocks at each end and a patch near the middle. If you are doing a longer swim, make sure you wear a tow float as it is a popular spot for paddleboards and small boats, although there is plenty of space for everyone.

TECHNICAL INFORMATION

DESCRIPTION **beach** ORIENTATION **south-east** TIDES **best at high tide, but possible at any time** ACCESS **100m walk along sandy path to beach** ENTRY **sand** GOOD FOR **sheltered swims; quick dips; longer swims** LOCAL GROUP **Tiree Polar Bears** LOCATION **56.4719, -6.8961**

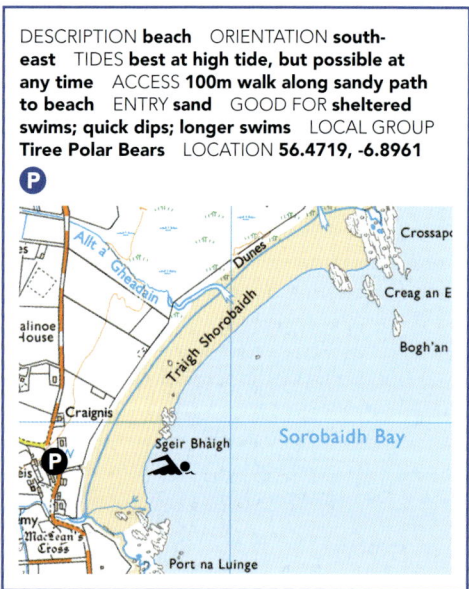

Getting there

Access to the beach is off the B8066. Follow signs to *Balemartine* and *Hynish*; there is a small parking area at the southern end of the beach, just after the turning signposted to *Balinoe*. Park just off the road, on the grass, opposite the sandy track down to the beach. There are no facilities.

Refreshments

» **Farmhouse Cafe**, Balemartine. Just a short walk along the lane from the beach. Great wee cafe with seating inside and outside. Highland cows, ponies and hungry chickens hoovering up the crumbs outside. Good coffee and cake, as well as hearty meals – perfect post-swim grub.

Torastan Beach, Coll

Coll is my favourite Inner Hebridean island – a perfect mixture of rugged landscape and turquoise waters, with lots of beaches and coves to explore. I love playing in the waves at the eastern end of Feall Bay, and finding otter prints across the sand at Sorisdale, but my favourite place to swim has to be the ever-changing Torastan Beach on the north-west coast.

Torastan Beach or Tràigh Gharbh (meaning 'Rough Beach') really changes character as the tide falls. At high tide, the beaches are small, with little islands scattered offshore, and it can be a bit exposed depending on the wind direction. At low tide, a series of safe, sheltered lagoons are revealed, with a narrow strip of sand (a tombolo) separating the bays. It is also a great place to look out for basking sharks, and you will almost certainly have a few seals keeping an eye on you as you swim.

THE SWIM

The best time to swim here is a couple of hours on either side of low tide, when there are several bays to choose from. The first horseshoe beach is sandy, shallow and usually very sheltered. I love swimming here in calm water and watching the waves crash against the rocks further out to sea. There are also several more swim options if you continue walking north-east along the shore.

This is a place for shorter swims in one or several of the small bays rather than longer swims. Always stick within the bays and do not venture out past the rocky islands, where there can be larger waves and stronger tidal currents.

1 Torastan Beach sheltered lagoon at low tide

TECHNICAL INFORMATION

DESCRIPTION **beach** ORIENTATION **north-west, with north-east and south-west-facing sections at low tide** TIDES **best a couple of hours after high tide** ACCESS **500m walk along a grassy track to the nearest part of beach** ENTRY **sand** GOOD FOR **sheltered swims; wildlife spotting; multiple dipping options** LOCATION **56.6705, -6.5359**

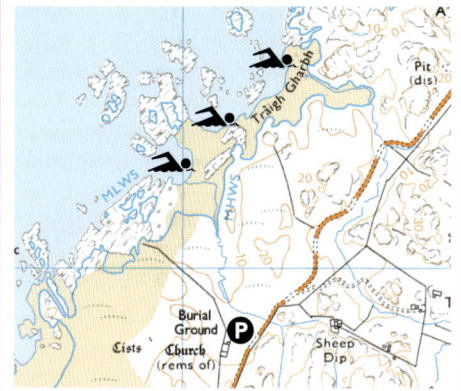

Getting there

Take the B8071 north out of Arinagour and then turn right on to the B8072. After around two kilometres, you will see a burial ground on the left. Parking is on the large grassy area by the burial ground. There are no facilities.

Access

Go through the gate with a sign saying *Torastan Farm, camping permitted with permission*. It's a ten-minute walk along the track, following the fence line on your left, down to the beach. You can swim at the first horseshoe bay or walk further along the beach to reach other lovely entry spots.

Refreshments

There is not a huge amount happening on Coll. There is just one cafe, one hotel and one shop in Arinagour … of course, I had to try them all out! As with anywhere remote, be sure to check opening hours and book ahead if you can.

» **Island Cafe**, Arinagour. Delicious food, good coffee and great hot, sticky cinnamon buns. As it's the only cafe on the island it can get busy, so call ahead to book if you can (especially around lunchtime). Seasonal.

» **Coll Hotel**, Arinagour. Outstanding locally sourced food and always a friendly welcome. Open to non-residents, but you will need to book ahead.

» **Coll Stores**, Arinagour. This is where you need to stock up on swim snacks! They also sell gin from the Isle of Coll Distillery.

SKYE & LOCHABER

Opposite River Etive © Alastair Goodridge

River Etive

Glen Etive (*Gleann Èite* in Gaelic) holds a special place in my heart. It is one of the first places I visited (and dipped in) in the Highlands before I moved here, and I'm sure its wild beauty influenced my decision to relocate here permanently. I've been back many times, exploring the best places to access the river and swimming in the gorgeous sea loch at the end of the long road that meanders through the glen.

The name Etive is believed to mean 'Little Fierce One' or 'Little Ugly One', referring to the Gaelic goddess associated with Loch Etive.

While the scenery is far from ugly, the river flow can be extremely fierce, especially during the spring snowmelt. In the summer, after a dry spell, the water in the river calms to a gentle flow. There are multiple waterfalls and deep pools to enjoy.

While there are many places to dip in the river (I think I've swum in about 14 different locations in total), I have selected a few of the best ones (running east to west, gradually heading downhill towards Loch Etive) in terms of parking, size, access and views. The first two spots can get busy on sunny days, as they are not far from the A82. If this is the case, it's worth continuing to the next spots along the glen.

TRIANGLE POOL

The first large pool on the river, around 300 metres after the Sheep Transporter bridge. It is triangular and deep, with a swimmable area around 20 metres wide and 30 metres long. Upstream there is a series of smaller pools and waterfalls (also known as the Triple Falls). These are swimmable when the river levels are low. They involve a bit of a scramble down the rocks to access.

UPPER POOL

The next pool is around 750 metres further down the river. Here the waterfall current splits into two, and there is a large deep pool, around 30 metres long. Although this is a gorgeous place to swim if the river is calm, be aware that there can be a moderately strong circular current at the far side of the pool.

LOWER POOL

Carry on along the road, past the area enclosed by deer fencing and a further 1.5 kilometres past the road bridge at Alltchaorunn, and you will come to a gorgeous pool with spectacular views of the knobbly summit of An Grianan. This is the most accessible pool, with no slopes or scrambling down rocks to get in. Parking limited.

GORGE

If you've made it this far (around nine kilometres from the junction with the A82), you're in for a real treat! This is my favourite spot to swim along the river. From the parking area on the bend, walk downstream and enter the river at a large pool; from here, you can swim upstream for the whole length of the gorge (around 80 metres) to the waterfalls at the top.

TECHNICAL INFORMATION

DESCRIPTION **river pools**   RIVER **Etive**   ELEVATION **Triangle Pool 165m; Upper Pool 150m; Lower Pool 95m; Gorge 90m**   ACCESS **varied – some scrambles down the rocks, some gentle slopes and pebbly beaches**   ENTRY **rocky/pebbly**   GOOD FOR **spectacular views; multiple waterfall pools; river exploring**   LOCATION **Triangle Pool 56.6252, -4.9061; Upper Pool 56.6220, -4.9151; Lower Pool 56.6160, -4.9604; Gorge 56.6159, -4.9687**

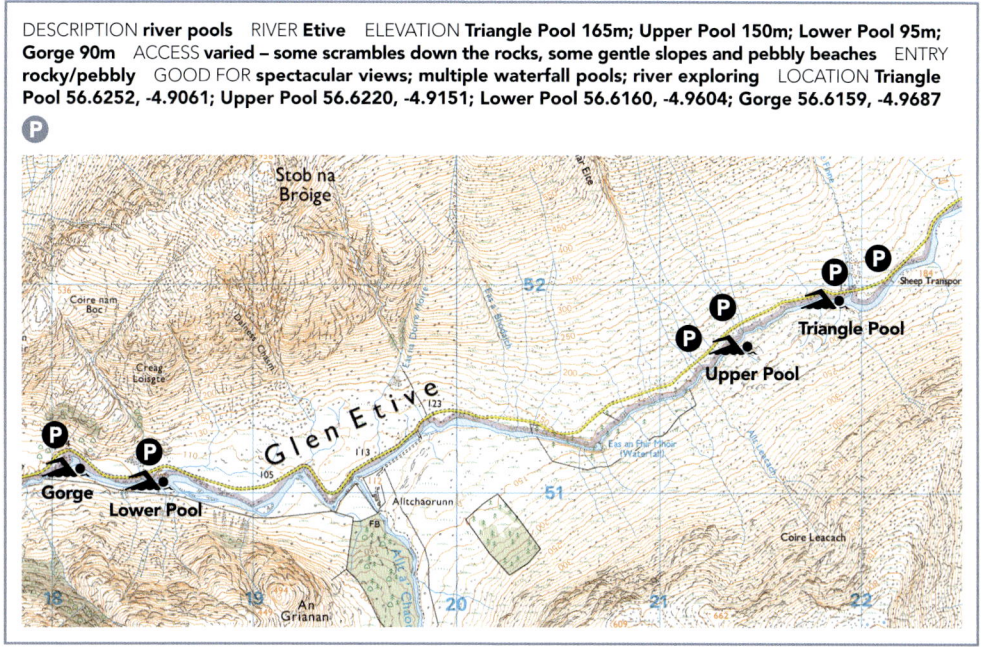

Getting there

Glen Etive is signed off the A82 between Glencoe and Bridge of Orchy. Each swimming spot has a small amount of lay-by parking. If one location is busy, then try moving on to the next. Please do not block the passing places as this will cause chaos.

River level information

Only consider swimming in the river when the water levels are low. There is no SEPA water level monitoring on this river; however, as this is a popular kayaking river, the Scottish Canoe Association recommends looking at the SEPA river levels of a nearby river, south-east of the Etive catchment (Linne nam Beathach @Victoria Bridge). Generally, the two rivers respond similarly to rain as they have similar catchment areas and topography. Of course, localised rainfall differences, particularly summer thunderstorms, may result in significant differences in level, but it will give you a good idea of what the levels are likely to be like. As always, assess the water level and conditions for yourself before swimming.

Refreshments

If you've travelled a long way down Glen Etive, it's a long way back up the road to the nearest pub or cafe. Take supplies and have a picnic or stop on your way back at one of the following places.

» **White Corries Cafe**, Glencoe Mountain Resort. Big modern cafe at the ski centre. Beautiful views with lots of parking.
» **The Way Inn**, Kingshouse Hotel, Glencoe. All that remains of the original Kingshouse Hotel, now converted into a walkers' bar. Muddy boots welcome and a great place to warm up by the roaring fire. Tasty pub food and snacks. It can get busy with West Highland Way walkers during the summer.
» **Clachaig Inn**, Glencoe. Great pub, popular with walkers and climbers. Excellent hot chocolate and cosy wood-burning stove. This place has a great atmosphere and often has live music in the evenings.

Loch Etive

Is it worth driving 20 kilometres along a narrow, single-track road to get to the loch at the end? Yes, absolutely! If you make the effort to get to Loch Etive, you will be rewarded with spectacular views and gorgeous water. I've been here many times, but somehow it always surprises me that this is a saltwater sea loch, complete with seaweed and crabs scuttling beneath the surface.

2 Seagull Island © Vivien Cumming

THE SWIM

The closest water to the car park is still the river; the best entry point for the loch is a bit further along. Follow the shore for around 200 metres before getting in. It is pretty gravelly underfoot, with sandy patches and occasional larger stones, and there is a nice gently sloping entry. The water is brackish, a mix of freshwater from the river and saltwater from the loch.

TECHNICAL INFORMATION

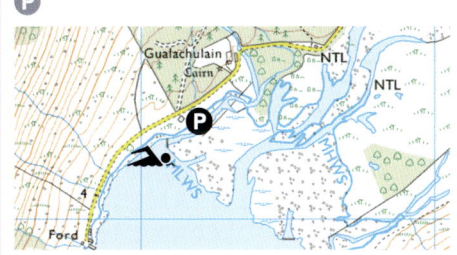

DESCRIPTION **sea loch** ORIENTATION **south-east**
TIDES **possible at any time** ACCESS **200m flat walk along stony, grassy shore** ENTRY **gravelly beach; gentle slope** GOOD FOR **amazing views; longer swims; picnics** LOCATION **56.5611, -5.0767**

Getting there

Glen Etive is signed off the A82 between Glencoe and Bridge of Orchy. The Loch Etive car park is around 20 kilometres from the junction with the A82. It is a tiny narrow road, so leave around an hour to get to the far end (allowing the same amount of time to get back again). The parking area is small, so make sure you avoid peak times on sunny days.

Refreshments

Either bring a picnic, or head back up to the A82 for pubs and cafes – there are some suggestions opposite.

Seagull Island, Loch Leven

Seagull Island, or *Eilean nam Ban* in Gaelic, is a small island at the Kinlochleven end of Loch Leven. As swimming spots go, it has one of the most iconic views in Scotland. Swimming out to the island, you can gaze across the water to the Aonach Eagach ridge and the pointy peak of Sgorr na Cìche, also known as the Pap of Glencoe, often reflected perfectly in the mirror-flat water.

Although it is called Seagull Island, I've seen many different types of birds here. In the spring, the island is often covered in geese, and some swans nest nearby. On my last visit, there were oystercatchers and curlews on the shore. Watch out for midges in the summer, as this area is infamous for them.

THE SWIM

The entry is stony and a bit seaweedy, with occasional larger rocks, but it does get deep enough to swim quite quickly. At high tide, it is just under 100 metres across to the island (less at low tide) and approximately 500 metres around the island and back to your starting point.

Watch out for jellyfish! It is sometimes easy to forget that you are in a sea loch as you are quite a way inland, but they do sometimes make an appearance.

TECHNICAL INFORMATION

DESCRIPTION **sea loch**   ORIENTATION **south-west**   TIDES **possible to swim at any time**   ACCESS **very close to the lay-by; small slope down to the rocky beach**   ENTRY **rocky; seaweedy**   GOOD FOR **incredible views; swims to the island**   LOCAL GROUP **Loch Leven (Glencoe) Wild Swimmers**   LOCATION **56.7134, -5.0065**

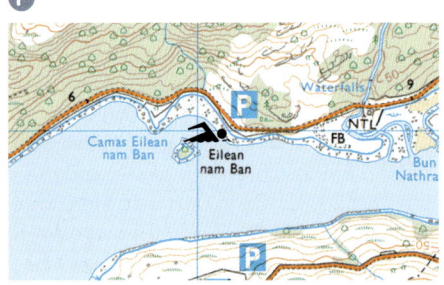

Getting there

Seagull Island is easily accessed from the B863, around three kilometres west of Kinlochleven. There is a large lay-by with space for around eight or ten cars. Please be aware that this is a popular parking place for camper vans and motorhomes, so it can get busy with larger vehicles. You can see the island from the lay-by.

Refreshments

» **Mo's**, Kinlochleven. Great little cafe with yummy breakfast rolls and cakes.
» **Bothy Bar**, Kinlochleven. This is the bar at the MacDonald Hotel, right next to the B863 on the way into Kinlochleven. Nothing fancy, but the bar meals are good.

Eas Chia-aig Waterfall

Eas Chia-aig (*Eas Chia-Bhalg* in Gaelic – possibly meaning 'Waterfall of the Bulge') is a mesmerising double waterfall with a deep plunge pool at the bottom. It was here that Liam Neeson leapt over the bridge to avoid being captured by the English in the 1995 Hollywood blockbuster *Rob Roy*.

I've been lucky enough to swim here on summer days when water levels have been low, and sunbeams danced through the water. I've also dipped here on cooler days when the flow has been a bit more feisty, but still safe enough to dunk. Stepping into the black, churning water, it is easy to understand why this waterfall also goes by the name of the Witches Cauldron. The surface of the water is restless and choppy, like swimming through a bubbling pot of tar – although somewhat colder than I would imagine that would feel.

THE SWIM

The entry to the pool is stony and, although initially quite shallow, gets deep around the base of the falls. The plunge pool is small, but there is enough room for a couple of people to swim. As tempting as it is, *do not jump in*. Someone visiting broke several bones in their foot while leaping off the rocks into the lower pool.

1 & 3 Eas Chia-aig Waterfall © Vivien Cumming   2 Above and below

TECHNICAL INFORMATION

DESCRIPTION **waterfall pool**   RIVER **Abhainn Chia-aig**   ELEVATION **50m**   ACCESS **150m walk along the road, followed by a steep path down to the pool**   ENTRY **stony**   GOOD FOR **dipping in the waterfall plunge pool**   LOCAL GROUP **Lochaber Loons**   LOCATION **56.9550, -5.0013**

Getting there

Take the A82 north out of Spean Bridge, then turn on to the B8004 towards Gairlochy. Continue on to the Gairlochy Swing Bridge over the Caledonian Canal and turn right after the bridge on to the B8005 to reach the Forestry Commission car park at Eas Chia-aig.

Access

To access the pool beneath the waterfall, walk along the road and on the far side of the bridge there is a steep little path on the right, taking you down to the stony beach area. If a strong flow of water runs across the shallow area before you get to the deeper pool, then the flow is too fast to swim. Leave it for another time and continue walking to Loch Arkaig (see overleaf) instead.

Refreshments

There are no options close by, so I would advise taking a flask and picnic. However, if you are craving hot food and drink, Spean Bridge isn't too far away and has a couple of places to eat.

» **The Bridge Cafe**, Spean Bridge. Basic but tasty. Everything you need for a post-swim refuel. I've stopped here many times on my way home from the west of Scotland.

» **Spean Bridge Mill Cafe**, Spean Bridge. Handy cafe at Spean Bridge Mill. Nothing fancy but good coffee and quick service (as long as a coach party has not just arrived).

Loch Arkaig

Loch Arkaig is a hidden gem and well worth a detour if you are staying in or around Fort William or travelling south from Inverness. Surrounding the loch is one of the UK's most extensive areas of ancient Caledonian pine forest. The landscape is remote, wild and wet; Loch Arkaig is surrounded by mountains and moorland, which provide a good range of habitats for local flora and fauna. These include spectacular 'granny' pines and rare bryophytes (mosses and liverworts), which are typical of 'Scotland's rainforest'. Look out for pine martens and red squirrels in the forest, and ospreys swooping over the loch.

I've enjoyed many swims here in multiple places. The eastern end of the loch is the most accessible and popular with local swimmers but, as you head west along the narrow road, it gets much quieter and more remote.

EASTERN END

The main entry point (that most of the local swimmers use) is by the jetty at the eastern end of the loch. Enter the loch at the gap in the wall before the jetty. There is a slight slope before it gets stony (protective footwear recommended), and it gets deep enough to swim by the time you are level with the end of the jetty.

From here, you can hug the northern bank and swim parallel to the shore, or it's around 300 metres across to the other side. Be mindful that there could be boats on the loch, and make sure that you wear a tow float. If you want a longer swim, it is just over two kilometres to swim a loop of the nearby island.

PEBBLY BEACH AND STONE WALKWAY

If you want a bit more of an adventure, there are several other entry spots further along the loch. The entries are all quite stony and get deep reasonably quickly. Bear in mind that the water level can vary and so may be different from one visit to the next, and sometimes the stone walkway is completely submerged.

TECHNICAL INFORMATION

DESCRIPTION **freshwater loch**   MAXIMUM DEPTH **91m**   LENGTH **19km**   MAXIMUM WIDTH **1.2km**
ELEVATION **45m**   ACCESS **Eastern End is a 700m walk along the road; Pebbly Beach and Stone Walkway
are next to roadside parking**   ENTRY **mostly gravelly/stony**   GOOD FOR **multiple entry points; amazing
views; refreshing dips; longer swims**   LOCAL GROUP **Lochaber Loons**   LOCATION **Eastern End 56.9540,
-5.0110; Pebbly Beach 56.9740, -5.1339; Stone Walkway 56.9811, -5.2082**

Eastern End

Pebbly Beach

Stone walkway

Getting there

Take the A82 north out of Spean Bridge, then
turn on to the B8004 towards Gairlochy. Continue
on to the Gairlochy Swing Bridge over the
Caledonian Canal and turn right after the bridge
on to the B8005 to reach the Forestry Commission
car park at Eas Chia-aig, at the eastern tip of
Loch Arkaig. Either park here for the Eastern End,
or continue along the northern shore of Loch
Arkaig to reach the roadside parking for the other
swimming spots. There is only space for a couple
of cars at the roadside parking; please do not
block entrances or passing places.

Access – Eastern End

From the car park at Eas Chia-aig, walk for

around 700 metres along the minor road until
you see the gap in the wall before you reach the
jetty. There is a small lay-by close to the entry,
but please be aware that people with boats use
this to access the water. Please be considerate
of other water users and don't park here unless
you are here very early or very late.

Access – Pebbly Beach and Stone Walkway

These swimming spots are easy to access and
only a few metres from the roadside parking.

Refreshments

There are no options close by. Either take a hot
drink and a snack or there are some ideas in
nearby Spean Bridge on page 27.

Sanna Bay, Ardnamurchan

Sanna Bay is one of my favourite places in Scotland. Remote and wild, the journey to get there is an adventure in itself. When you drive along the narrow road from Kilchoan to Sanna, you pass through a low-lying, almost moon-like terrain fringed on all sides by lumpy black hills. You are, in fact, travelling through the magma chamber of an extinct volcano.

With its rugged backdrop of dark volcanic hills, views across to the Small Isles, white shell sand, turquoise waters and towering sand dunes, Sanna Bay is a beautiful place to dip, explore the rock pools and marvel at the wild beauty of the Ardnamurchan peninsula. Look out for otters, sea eagles and the occasional Highland cow on the beach.

THE SWIM

I've swum here many times, in all conditions. The beauty of this jagged coastline is that there is almost always a sheltered place to dip.

The northernmost beach is lovely at high tide – sheltered from most directions and with reasonably shallow sea across to Sanna Island. At low tide, you can walk to the island. Although you can't see it from the beach, if you swim out far enough, you can see around the corner to Ardnamurchan Lighthouse.

The next bay is bigger and gets deeper more quickly – it is great for longer swims. At high tide, you can swim around the island in the middle (this is around 400 metres if you start at the top of the beach), or it's around 300 metres (one way) if you swim the length of the beach, parallel to the shore. Watch out for submerged rocks.

If the wind is blowing directly in from the west, then the little south-facing cove is your best bet for calm water.

TECHNICAL INFORMATION

DESCRIPTION **beach**   ORIENTATION **west**
TIDES **better at high tide but possible to swim at any time**   ACCESS **approximately 400m walk on sandy track through the dunes; steep in places**   ENTRY **sand**   GOOD FOR **sheltered swims; pottering around the bays; spectacular views**   LOCATION **56.7450, -6.1834**

Getting there

Driving or cycling to Sanna Bay are the only options, and it's not for the faint-hearted! It is a long way from anywhere, and the roads are very narrow and winding.

From Kilchoan, look out for the signpost to *Sanna*, and then turn right again before Kilchoan Fire Station for the last seven kilometres of single-track road to the Sanna Bay car park. There are no facilities.

Access

To access the closest part of the beach, follow the small sandy tracks through the dunes. All paths lead to the beach, although some tracks are steeper than others.

1 Sanna Bay 2 Sanna Bay © Anna Deacon 3 Camusdarach Beach

I usually start by heading to the northern-most bay. The quickest way to get there is to take the vehicle track north from the car park, towards the houses, and then skirt around the far side of the dunes to get to the beach. There are also plenty of small tracks through the dunes to get to the other parts of the beach.

Refreshments

» **The Stables Coffee Shop**, Ardnamurchan Point. I always try to combine my swims at Sanna Bay with a trip to Ardnamurchan Point for a hot drink and a traybake in the cafe. There is also a little gift shop and beautiful views if the weather is nice enough to sit outside. Seasonal.

» **Puffin Coffee**, Kilchoan. Lovely friendly cafe at the community centre. Excellent cakes, coffee and hot chocolate.

Camusdarach Beach

I head west to Arisaig every year in early December for some pre-Christmas winter sea swimming. At this time of year, the water is chilly, but the beaches are lovely and quiet, and it's a time for spectacular sunsets, spiced hot chocolate and mince pies on the beach.

With its views over to the jagged Cuillin Ridge on Skye, the rugged peaks of Rùm and the steep sea cliffs of Eigg, Camusdarach Beach is a swimmer's dream. The Main Beach is sheltered from the south and south-west and is a wonderful place to dunk, play in the gentle waves and soak up the views. It can get busy in the summer as there is a campsite by the beach, but the limited parking and vast expanse of sand means that it is never as crowded as some other local beaches.

THE SWIM

The Main Beach is excellent for longer swims parallel to the shore, particularly at low tide. At low water, the beach expands, and the little bays to the south connect, giving you a 500-metre stretch of sand to the south, so longer swims are possible too. At high tide, the first section of the beach is around 300 metres long.

The West Beach is smaller, only around 50 metres across, but is a perfect place to watch the sunset over the islands. I've mostly swum here in the winter when the wind has been blowing relentlessly from the north, making the Main Beach unsafe for swimming. It is a gorgeous spot and usually much quieter than the larger Main Beach.

TECHNICAL INFORMATION

DESCRIPTION **beach**   ORIENTATION **north-west and south-west**   TIDES **possible to swim at any time**   ACCESS **350m sandy track to the Main Beach; further to the West Beach (tide dependent)**   ENTRY **sand**   GOOD FOR **playing in the waves; longer swims; spectacular island views**   LOCATION **Main Beach 56.9588, -5.8487; West Beach 56.9556, -5.8534**

Getting there

Parking for Camusdarach Beach is at Glenancross, on the small coastal road (B8008) between Arisaig and Mòrar. The car park is reasonably small and has a height restriction bar. Make sure you get there early during busy times as it fills up quickly. There are no other facilities.

Access

From the car park, follow the little path over the bridge and immediately turn right. The path follows the burn through the dunes before emerging at the northern end of the Main Beach.

If the tide is out, you can walk along the beach and over the dunes to get to the West Beach. If the tide is high, you need to take an alternative route to the West Beach. From the car park, cross the bridge and carry on straight ahead up the slope and follow inland tracks for around one kilometre to the beach.

Refreshments

» **The Bakehouse & Crannog**, Mallaig. The best artisan bakery in the area. Delicious sourdough breads, pastries and cakes. Great coffee too. The Crannog also serves pizzas on Saturday evenings.
» **The Cabin**, Mallaig. Small but perfectly formed. Excellent fish and chips. Seasonal.
» **Arisaig Shellfish Shack**, Arisaig. If you love seafood, you will love this little shack! Limited opening hours, but top-quality food and well worth a visit. If you are staying locally, they also have a bread shed, where you can pre-order pastries, bread and pizzas for collection. Seasonal.

1 Ord, Skye © Alastair Goodridge

Ord Beach, Skye

Ord is a little hamlet on the north-west coast of the Sleat peninsula, with beautiful views across Loch Eishort to Blàbheinn and the Black Cuillin. I came across this little beach by chance when staying nearby and couldn't resist a swim. I loved it so much I had to go back again!

THE SWIM

The swimmable part of the beach is directly opposite the stone ramp; at mid tide there is a sandy entry with a few seaweedy rocks. There is a lovely, sheltered channel to swim in, protected by the skerries, and there are often small boats or buoys 50 or 100 metres out to swim around.

TECHNICAL INFORMATION

DESCRIPTION **beach** ORIENTATION **north-west** TIDES **better around mid tide** ACCESS **ramp or grassy walk down to the beach** ENTRY **sandy; can be a few rocks and seaweed** GOOD FOR **dramatic scenery; sheltered swims** LOCATION **57.1481, -5.9423**

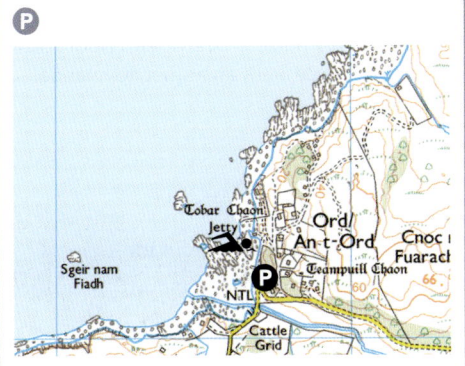

Getting there

From the A851 Broadford–Armadale road, take the turning to Ord (signposted) and follow the single-track road for about seven kilometres until you reach the bay.

There is an obvious gravelled area with room for cars to park next to the beach. This gives easy access to the beach, either over the grass and stones or down the stone ramp (north of the parking area). Parking is limited, but it has never been too busy when I have visited.

Refreshments

» **Torabhaig Distillery Cafe**, Sleat. Cosy cafe with great hot chocolate. Not open at weekends.
» **The Cafe**, An Crùbh, Sleat. An Crùbh (Gaelic for 'The Hub') is a community cafe and shop. Yummy baking, including flapjacks, cakes and scones.

1 Cassie and the magical water of the Fairy Pools © Susanne Masters **2** Early morning dip in the Upper Pool

Fairy Pools, Skye

'Have you been to the Fairy Pools on Skye?' is a question I get asked regularly.

With crystal-clear water cascading into shimmering blue-green pools, all surrounded by an amphitheatre of jagged ridges, it's easy to see why the Fairy Pools have become the most famous, high-on-the-wish-list, wild swimming destination in Scotland.

As a fair warning, the Fairy Pools are not only popular with swimmers. Due to a crazy amount of media hype over the last few years, the pools are now one of Skye's most popular tourist hot spots, attracting hundreds of tourists daily at busy times. Unfortunately, they have been a victim of their own success – too picturesque, too accessible, too Instagrammable. During the summer months, the car park is chock-a-block by 9 a.m. Even in winter, the place is swarming by mid-morning.

So, have I put you off yet? Thankfully, things are improving, and recent investment and ongoing infrastructure upgrades (parking, toilet facilities, path improvements, and so on) mean that the crowds can be managed more sustainably, but it is still very busy.

I'm pleased to say that if you don't mind getting up at sparrow's fart, then it is still possible to have a quiet swim away from the crowds so that you can experience a little bit of the Fairy Pools magic for yourself. Being an early bird myself, I prefer to get there at the beginning of the day, and I've found that between 6 a.m. and 8 a.m. is the sweet spot in the summer (but, honestly, the earlier the better). Late evening dips are also possible.

THE SWIM

There are so many beautiful pools along this section of river, some more accessible than others. I've swum in lots of them, and I have selected my two favourite pools to share with you. The Upper Pool is a slightly longer walk but is more accessible once you're there. The Lower Pool is a bit of a scramble but 100 per cent worth it! Please be aware that all the entries are rocky and can be slippery when wet. Grippy wetsuit boots or shoes (rather than neoprene socks) are recommended.

The Lower Pool is a lovely deep pool above a double cascade, with an adjoining channel

leading to another waterfall. This was the first place I ever swam at the Fairy Pools, and it's still my favourite. It is around 1.2 kilometres along the path from the car park, just above an underwater arch. It is a short scramble down to get in, but manageable with grippy footwear and a bit of a bum shuffle along the rocks.

The underwater arch pool adjoining the Lower Pool may be very tempting to try and get down to, but it isn't accessible without risking your safety. I have swum in this pool myself, but it is one heck of a scramble down a slippery, near-vertical rock face. So, I would stick to the pool just above, which is safer and, in my opinion, much nicer.

If you continue up the path for another 300 metres from the Lower Pool, you'll find the more accessible Upper Pool. It's only big enough for about three strokes of front crawl but perfect for a refreshing dip and relaxing float.

TECHNICAL INFORMATION

DESCRIPTION **river pool**   RIVER **Allt Coir' a' Mhadaidh**   ELEVATION **Lower Pool 90m; Upper Pool 140m**   ACCESS **1.2km to Lower Pool; 1.5km to Upper Pool; good track (uphill); muddy at edges**   ENTRY **rocky; steep entry to Lower Pool**   GOOD FOR **bucket-list swims; crystal clear water; spectacular scenery**   LOCATION **Upper Pool 57.2493, -6.2499; Lower Pool 57.2498, -6.2550**   AVOID **between 9 a.m. and 8 p.m. in summer; slightly less busy in winter but still go early or late to avoid the crowds**

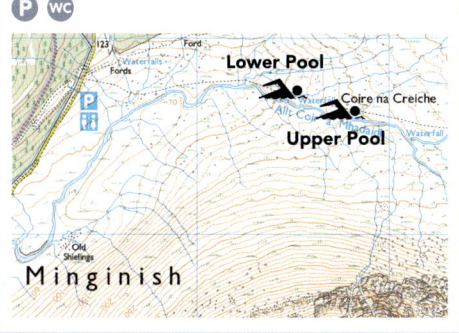

Getting there

Take the B8009 west towards Carbost and turn off at Merkadale on to a single-track road, signposted *Glen Brittle*. The road passes through Glen Brittle Forest to reach the Fairy Pools car park on your right (pay and display). The car park has been expanded in recent years, but still fills up incredibly quickly. There are toilet facilities in the car park.

In the summer there is a bus service from Portree that drops you in the car park, but the timetable means that you will struggle to avoid the crowds if you take this option.

From the car park, cross the road and follow the path down the hill and then uphill towards the river pools. The track is generally good, but there are some muddy parts, so ensure you have suitable footwear.

Refreshments

» **Cuillin Coffee Co**., Glenbrittle Campsite. Looks like a tin shed but actually serves the *best* coffee on Skye. Lovely cosy cafe, excellent hot chocolate, smoothies and pastries. Fabulous lunch menu and fresh bread. Seasonal.

» **Café Cùil**, Satran. Delicious brunch and lunch options with a great selection of cakes. Modern and busy with lots of space inside and outside. Seasonal.

Talisker Bay, Skye

With its rocky outcrops, clear water, towering cliffs and dramatic waterfall plunging into the sea, Talisker Bay holds a special place in my heart. My husband and I love this place so much (along with the whisky) that we named our old dog Talisker, and I have so many wonderful memories of her bounding along this beautiful beach.

The name Talisker derives from either the Scottish Gaelic *Talamh Sgeir*, meaning 'Land of the Cliff', or the Norse *t-Hallr Skjaer*, which means 'Sloping Rock'. Either way, it is a dramatic landscape and a wonderful place to swim when the conditions allow. I love the zigzag patterns of black and white sand, creating a marbled effect along the beach and under the water – make sure you take your goggles.

THE SWIM

The entry here is best at low tide, as you have plenty of beautiful sand to walk over and a nice, gently sloping entry. At mid tide, it's a mixture of sand and stones and, by high tide, the waves break up on the rocks, and it isn't easy getting in or out.

On all my visits here, I have opted to potter about rather than swim any great distance. I prefer marvelling at the scenery above and below the water and bobbing about in the waves. However, the bay is around 500 metres across, so it is suitable for longer swims in calm conditions.

TECHNICAL INFORMATION

DESCRIPTION **beach**   ORIENTATION **west**   TIDES **best at low tide**   ACCESS **1.5km flat walk along a good track to the beach; rocky section before sand**   ENTRY **sandy/stony**   GOOD FOR **dramatic scenery; sunset swims; playing in the waves**   LOCATION **57.2831, -6.4587**

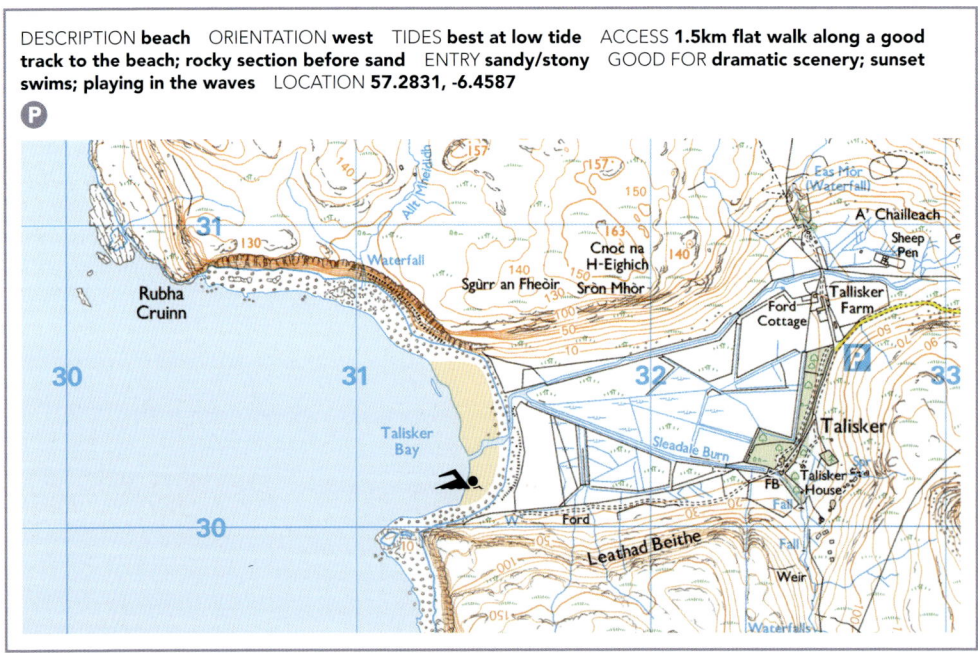

1 Talisker Bay © Shutterstock/Harald Schmidt

Getting there

From Carbost, head west on the small no-through road, signposted *Talisker*. From here it is around seven kilometres to the parking area. Parking is on either side of the road, just before the public road ends, and is extremely limited. It is best to try and get here early or late in the day in the summer months. I have found it much quieter outside main holiday times.

Notes

On a recent visit, I was sad to see quite a bit of plastic washed up on the shore after a recent storm. Please consider taking a bag with you and picking up what you can to protect this otherwise pristine place.

Refreshments

» **Caora Dhubh Coffee Company**, Carbost. Caora Dhubh (from the Gaelic for 'Black Sheep') is directly opposite Talisker Distillery. It has exceptional coffee and a great selection of cakes. Keep an eye out for seals and otters in the bay while drinking your coffee.
» **The Old Inn**, Carbost. Hearty pub grub with good vegetarian options and local ales.

Claigan Coral Beach, Skye

Look carefully at Claigan Coral Beach's dazzling white sand, and you'll find it isn't sand (or coral) at all. Instead, the beach consists of sun-bleached skeletons of a red coralline seaweed known as maërl. Rarely for a seaweed, maërl grows a hard outer skeleton by depositing calcium carbonate in its cell walls. There are also immeasurable quantities of broken-up shells.

Make sure you bring your goggles when you swim here. With perfectly clear water, black volcanic rocks and dazzling white maërl sand, it's easy to imagine you are on a tropical island, except the sea is a lot colder!

THE SWIM

High tide is the ideal time to swim as the entry is mainly sandy, and there is a lovely, sheltered strip of water between the beach and the island of Lampay to potter around in. There are still a few stones underfoot as you get in, so I recommend wearing something protective on your feet.

At mid tide, swimming in reasonably shallow water is possible, but more of the stones are exposed, and the entry is a bit trickier. At high tide, it is just under 200 metres across to the nearest point of the island. At low tide, you can walk across the bay to the island.

Seals are often spotted in the water as the small rocky islands and quiet shores around Dunvegan are breeding grounds for common seals. Make sure you keep your distance.

TECHNICAL INFORMATION

DESCRIPTION **beach**   ORIENTATION **west**
TIDES **best at high tide**   ACCESS **1.8km walk along a good track to the beach**   ENTRY **sandy/ stony**   GOOD FOR **clear water; sheltered swims; wildlife spotting**   LOCATION **57.5011, -6.6380**
AVOID **peak times**

Getting there

From Dunvegan, head towards Dunvegan Castle on the A850 then continue along a single-track road for 5.5 kilometres until you get to Claigan Coral Beach car park. The road is very narrow and not suitable for long vehicles and motorhomes. This is a very popular spot and parking is limited, so make sure you avoid peak times – before 10 a.m. and after 7 p.m. seem to be OK in the summer. It isn't as crowded in the winter. There are no facilities at the car park.

1 Claigan Coral Beach © Shutterstock/Lukassek 2 Black rocks and white maërl sand 3 Shells and maërl

Access

The 1.8-kilometre path to the beach is well signed from the car park. The path is generally good, with some gentle ups and downs. Comfortable, sturdy footwear is essential.

Refreshments

» **MacLeod Tables Cafe**, Dunvegan Castle. Located in the Dunvegan Castle car park (free parking). Good, simple food and an excellent selection of cakes. Seasonal.

» **Jann's**, Dunvegan. Tiny organic cafe with a huge selection of home-made cakes and chocolates. Generous portions. Amazing Belgian hot chocolate, coffee, toasties and Caribbean-style curries. Can get busy at peak times.

OUTER HEBRIDES

Opposite West Beach, Berneray

Vatersay

Vatersay is a sea swimmer's dream! With two outstanding beaches on opposite sides of an isthmus, there is always somewhere sheltered to swim.

TRÀIGH A BHAIGH

The east-facing beach is generally very sheltered and a popular anchorage for sailing boats. If you are lucky enough to be there on a sunny day, the water here rivals any tropical island paradise. It can be so tempting that even people who don't usually swim in the sea might be persuaded to come in for a dip – although they may be put off when they realise the water is just as cold as everywhere else in this part of Scotland.

Tràigh a Bhaigh is usually the best of the two beaches for swimming. The bay is protected from all angles, apart from when the wind blows directly from the east.

There are sometimes cows on the beach, but they are completely unbothered by people and usually keep to themselves at one end of the beach or hide in the dunes. You can get in anywhere along the beach, and there are no strong currents. This is a lovely place for a long swim along the shore (700 metres each way), a pootle around the moored boats or just a quick dunk before your cake at the cafe.

Make sure you are visible when swimming here, and keep clear of the jetty at the far southern end of the beach.

TRÀIGH SIAR

The west-facing beach is more exposed and wild, but still stunning. On the walk through the dunes, you pass the monument to those killed in the *Annie Jane* shipwreck in 1853. There are also remains of a circular fortified dwelling house, or dun, at the southern end of the beach. The dun forms part of a string of sites of similar structures found along the west coast of the islands, built by the Celts around 2,000 years ago.

Tràigh Siar is a bit stonier than Tràigh a Bhaigh, with some pebbly areas, and is only suitable for swimming if the waves are spilling gently (rather than crashing on to the shore). Stick close to the shore and stay away from the rocky edges as there can be currents. It's a very long way to walk out to the sea at low tide, but still worth it for a quick splash in the waves if the conditions allow you to dip on both sides.

TECHNICAL INFORMATION

DESCRIPTION **beach** ORIENTATION **east (Tràigh a Bhaigh); west (Tràigh Siar)** TIDES **best at high tide; Tràigh a Bhaigh swimmable at any time** ACCESS **short walk from parking by the community hall, or a steeper, sandy path through the dunes from the main car park** ENTRY **sand** GOOD FOR **two beaches to choose from; quick dips; splashing in the waves; longer swims** LOCATION **Tràigh a Bhaigh 56.9246, -7.5342; Tràigh Siar 56.9254, -7.5455**

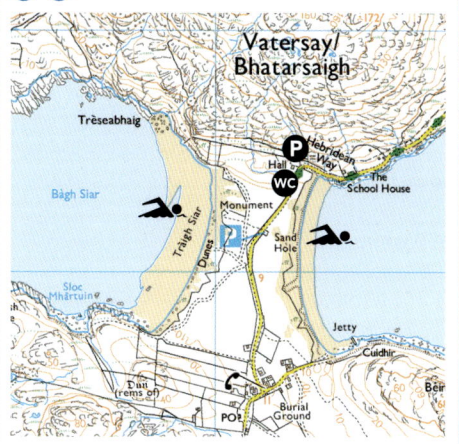

Getting there

Cross over the causeway to Vatersay and follow the 'main' road until you reach Vatersay community hall and cafe. You can either park here or continue for a couple of hundred metres along the road, where there is additional car parking. Then follow tracks through the dunes to get to the beaches on either side.

Refreshments

» **Vatersay Community Hall Cafe**, Vatersay. Friendly community cafe. Simple tasty food, hot drinks, cake and ice creams. Seasonal. Cash only when I last visited. There are also public toilets and showers at the community hall.

Eoligarry Beach, Barra

Barra is blessed with many incredible beaches. Those on the west coast are generally exposed to Atlantic swell and dangerous currents. On one occasion, I was met by the biggest swarm of compass jellyfish I had ever seen, washed on to a beach near Castlebay. Although this is a rare occurrence (the jellyfish had cleared entirely a week later), it caused me to explore the vast beaches of Barra's northern peninsula.

Most of the beaches here are massive and not great for swimming, being extremely shallow at high tide and too far to walk to the water at low tide. Tràigh Mhòr (meaning 'Big Beach') is so huge that it is used as the runway for the local airport. It is the only tidal beach runway in the world operating commercial scheduled flights.

The two smaller bays on either side of Eoligarry Harbour are an exception. They are easy to access, and get deep enough to swim pretty quickly. Although definitely best around at high tide, there are even some swimmable pockets of water when the tide is lower. Overlooking the island of Fuday, with South Uist and Eriskay in the far distance, they are beautiful, peaceful places to swim. And not a jellyfish in sight, despite the swarms I experienced towards the south of the island!

THE SWIM

I prefer the North Beach as it gets deep enough to swim more quickly and isn't so far to walk out to the water when the tide is slightly out. It is a small bay, only around 150 metres across. The South Beach is also lovely for a dip but best at high tide when it is pretty shallow, but usually lovely and sheltered. Both beaches have nice sandy entries.

Stick within the bays and be mindful of the harbour entrance at the lower end of the North Beach (tow floats essential).

TECHNICAL INFORMATION

DESCRIPTION **beach**   ORIENTATION **east**
TIDES **best around high tide**   ACCESS **short walk to each beach along a track; stream crossing for South Beach**   ENTRY **sand**   GOOD FOR **sheltered swims; quick dips; crystal-clear water**
LOCATION **North Beach 57.0434, -7.4200; South Beach 57.0407, -7.4216**   AVOID **harbour entrance at the lower end of the North Beach**

Getting there

Eoligarry (Eòlaigearraidh) is on the northernmost peninsula of Barra, north of the airport. Once you get to Eoligarry village, take one of the roads towards the east coast to reach the small parking area at Eoligarry Harbour.

From the car park, either take the track to the North Beach or one of the small grass tracks to the South Beach.

Notes

If you would like more information on safe swimming locations on Barra, I suggest popping into **Bùth Bharraigh** in Castlebay. It's a wonderful shop and community-led social enterprise and, as several keen swimmers work there, they may be able to point you towards their favourite local spots.

Refreshments

» **Ardmhor Coffee**, Ardmhor Ferry Terminal. Tiny little takeaway cafe with a staggering array of delicious cakes inside the wooden ferry waiting room. Excellent coffee. You can choose between classic, chilli and coconut or gingerbread hot chocolate – what more could you want?

» **Hebridean Toffee**, Castlebay. Toffee factory and cafe. A box of their toffee makes a great post-swim snack – seriously sugary, but perfect after a chilly sea swim.

Coilleag a' Phrionnsa, Eriskay

Coilleag a' Phrionnsa – the 'Prince's Cockleshell Strand' in Gaelic, also known as Prince's Beach – is said to be where Bonnie Prince Charlie first set foot on Scottish soil. From here, it is thought that he proceeded to Glenfinnan to make his first attempt at taking the crown in the Jacobite Rebellion of 1745.

It is a beautiful place to swim, with crystal-clear water and views across to the island of Lingeigh (meaning 'Heather Island') and the Sound of Barra. If you are taking the ferry to or from Barra, I advise scheduling some extra time for a dip at this beach.

THE SWIM

You can swim anywhere along the beach at any time. The northern stretch of the beach (above the rocky section) is just under 600 metres long, making it an excellent place for a longer swim parallel to the shore.

Although the beach is safe, being so close to the harbour (where the ferries to Barra arrive and depart, along with several smaller boats) means that you must wear a tow float when swimming here.

Please be aware that there is no clear barrier in the water between this beach and the harbour, so be careful not to cross into this area,

even if it is the calmest water on the day. I've seen paddleboarders get pushed down the beach by the wind and not realise they are entering the ferry lanes.

TECHNICAL INFORMATION

DESCRIPTION **beach** ORIENTATION **west** TIDES **can swim at any time** ACCESS **100m walk on path down to the beach** ENTRY **sand** GOOD FOR **pre- or post-ferry dips; long swims along the shore; turquoise water** LOCATION **57.0734, -7.3055** AVOID **harbour at south-west end of beach**

1 **Clachan Sands** © Annie Dunford   2 **Sunrise at Tràigh Hòrnais** © Alastair Goodridge
3 **Crystal-clear waters** © Susanne Masters

Getting there

Eriskay is between South Uist (to the north) and Barra (to the south). There is a lay-by for the beach (next to where a track runs down to the beach), which is around 200 metres from the ferry terminal, where ferries run to Barra. There is extra parking, toilets and showers by the ferry terminal.

Refreshments

» **Eriskay Community Shop**, Balla. Friendly little local shop selling all sorts of useful stuff. Not a cafe, but it has a wee tea and coffee station if you are looking for hot drinks. No inside seating but there are some benches outside.

» **Am Politician**, Balla. Named after the stricken vessel *SS Politician*, which ran aground off Eriskay in 1941. Serves meals all day. Reduced hours in winter.

» **Kilbride Cafe**, West Kilbride, South Uist. Great little cafe, with an adjoining campsite and hostel, right opposite its own little beach (which is one of my favourites, and great for a bonus swim). Simple, tasty food and hot drinks. Seasonal.

Clachan Sands, North Uist

There are two fantastic beaches at Clachan Sands – Tràigh Lingeigh to the north and Tràigh Hòrnais to the south. Both are relatively sheltered, making them great places to enjoy the water. If the conditions are calm, the rocks at the point between the two beaches are lovely for snorkelling at high tide.

TRÀIGH LINGEIGH

This beautiful, shallow bay overlooks the island of Lingeigh. With the rising and falling of the tides, the colour of the water here is ever-changing, from emerald and turquoise to opalescent.

This beach is a lovely place to paddle in shallow water at high tide. At low tide, it is an extra 300-metre walk to find water to swim in. Please note that the tide rises up the beach very quickly. I have also occasionally seen kite surfers using this beach, but only on days with a northwesterly wind.

TRÀIGH HÒRNAIS

On the other side of the small headland, Tràigh Hòrnais is a longer beach backed by magnificent machair-covered dunes. The water here is a deeper blue and is excellent for longer swims along the shore.

This is a narrower stretch of sand and is the beach to head to if you want to swim rather than just paddle. The entry is less affected by the tide and gets deep enough to swim more quickly. You can get in anywhere along Tràigh Hòrnais, and there is a good kilometre stretch before you hit the Trumisgarry inlet, where it starts to get too shallow to swim.

TECHNICAL INFORMATION

Getting there

Clachan Sands is at the northern end of North Uist, around seven kilometres from Berneray, where you can catch the ferry to Harris. Join the B893 either from Berneray to the north or from the A865 to the south.

Turn off the B893 beside a modern wooden house, signposted *Clachan Sands Cemetery* and *Beach Access*. (There is another turning signposted *Clachan Sands* just south of this one, but it takes you to some houses, not directly to the beach.)

Follow the road (which becomes more like a track) for around 800 metres until you reach a cemetery, where you can park before walking to the beach. If you continue along the track past

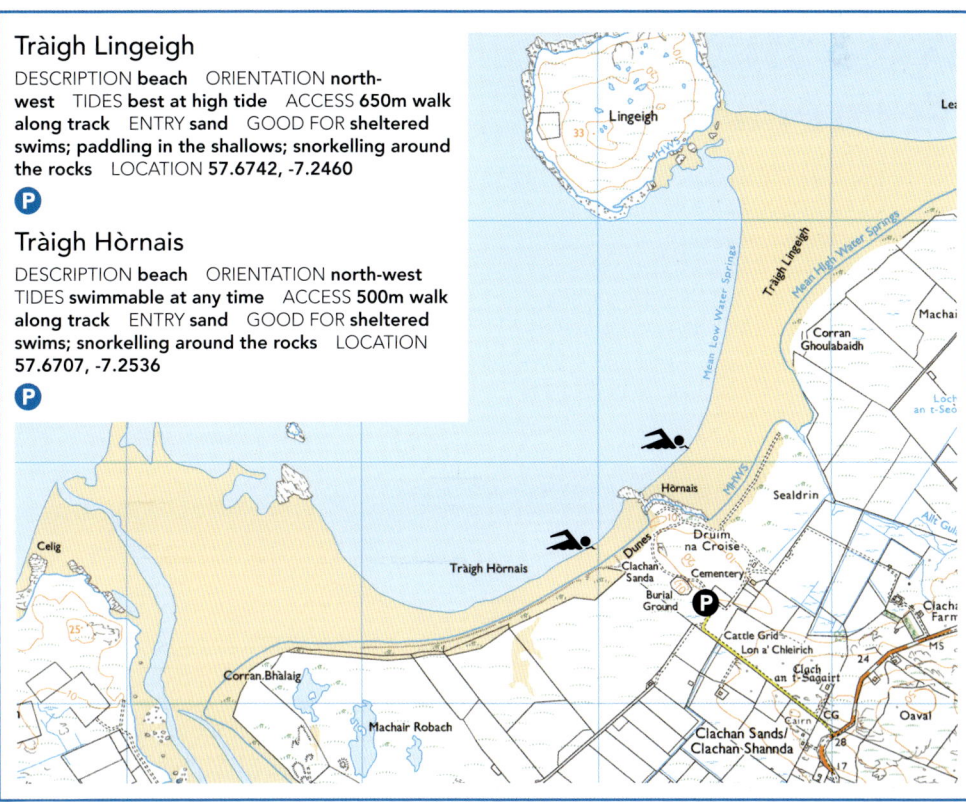

Tràigh Lingeigh

DESCRIPTION **beach**   ORIENTATION **north-west**   TIDES **best at high tide**   ACCESS **650m walk along track**   ENTRY **sand**   GOOD FOR **sheltered swims; paddling in the shallows; snorkelling around the rocks**   LOCATION **57.6742, -7.2460**

Tràigh Hòrnais

DESCRIPTION **beach**   ORIENTATION **north-west**   TIDES **swimmable at any time**   ACCESS **500m walk along track**   ENTRY **sand**   GOOD FOR **sheltered swims; snorkelling around the rocks**   LOCATION **57.6707, -7.2536**

another cemetery, there is an informal camping area with no facilities (apart from a rubbish bin and a water hose). Payment for camping is via a donation box.

Refreshments

Closest options are on Berneray (see opposite). There are also a couple of options elsewhere on North Uist.

» **The Wee Cottage Kitchen**, Malacleit. Great little food truck serving breakfast rolls, sandwiches, excellent home bakes and hot drinks. Seasonal.
» **Taigh Chearsabhagh Cafe**, Lochmaddy. Lovely cafe, shop and arts centre in Lochmaddy.

West Beach, Berneray

From my first peek of the turquoise water through the dunes, I fell in love with Berneray's West Beach. Berneray has a rich history for such a small island, and its natural habitats support varied and abundant wildlife. Look out for otter tracks in the sand and Arctic terns nesting in the dunes.

The beach has some of the clearest sea water I have ever had the pleasure to swim in; when I visited I had to pinch myself and remind myself that I was in Scotland, not the Caribbean!

I'm not the only one to think this beach looks more tropical than its location would suggest. In 2009, a Thai resort used a picture of the beach to promote their local beach, Kai Bae Beach. The rounded hills of Harris in the distance gave the game away. Of course, I am aware that I have visited in good weather and that it doesn't always look like a holiday brochure, but if you catch it under blue skies, there is nowhere quite like it.

THE SWIM

From the car park, follow the sandy track up through the machair and over the dunes to the beach.

The entry is sandy and gently sloping, and you can get in anywhere along the beach. I have only ever pottered about here, marvelling at the clarity of the water. The west-facing section of the beach is over three kilometres long, meaning that longer swims parallel to the beach are also possible.

As with many beaches in the Outer Hebrides, ensure you keep close to the shore to avoid tidal currents between the islands.

2 Miles of white sand, West Beach

TECHNICAL INFORMATION

DESCRIPTION **beach**   ORIENTATION **north-west**   TIDES **can swim at any time**   ACCESS **500m walk along track and through dunes to the beach**   ENTRY **sand**   GOOD FOR **long swims; quick dips; turquoise water; pretending you are in the Caribbean – or Thailand!**   LOCATION **57.7128, -7.2201**

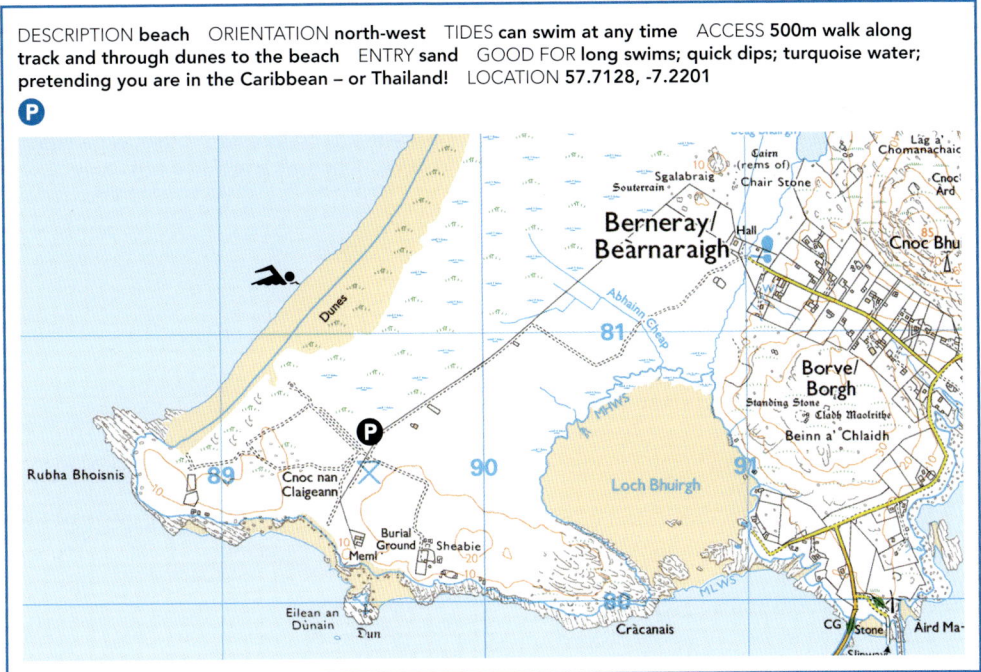

Getting there

Cross the causeway to Berneray from North Uist and take the first right. Follow the road past the Berneray Shop & Bistro and take the next left, signposted *Borve* and *Community Hall*. Once you pass the hall, continue over the cattle grid and follow the brown parking and picnic signs. It is around 1.8 kilometres further along the road (or track in places) to the small car park for the beach. There are picnic benches but no other facilities.

Refreshments

» **Berneray Shop & Bistro**, Borve. Handy little local shop and restaurant. The shop is open all year; check the opening hours of the restaurant before you travel.
» **Berneray Hot Plate**, Berneray Ferry Terminal. A food truck by the ferry terminal and a great place to grab early morning breakfast rolls or hot drinks. Opening times tend to coincide with ferry departures.

1 Horgabost Beach with Luskentyre in the background © Walkhighlands

Horgabost Beach, Harris

Protected by the Àird Niosaboist headland, Horgabost is another spectacular beach popular with local year-round swimmers. It has beautiful views back towards Luskentyre and over the Sound of Taransay. It is a smaller beach than Luskentyre, but it is generally safe and sheltered for swimming. I had a magical experience swimming here and seeing a porpoise swimming along a little further offshore.

THE SWIM

The beach has a gently sloping entry and is sandy the whole way along. It stays shallow for a long time at the western end of the beach, meaning you might be wading out for a while if you get in there.

This is generally a safe place to swim at any stage of the tide, although it is quite a walk (200 metres or so) out to the sea when the tide is low. Be careful around the far eastern side of the beach as some eddies can be caused by waves crashing around the rocks.

TECHNICAL INFORMATION

DESCRIPTION **beach**   ORIENTATION **north**
TIDES **can swim at any time**   ACCESS **car park by beach; 200m walk across sand at low tide**
ENTRY **sand**   GOOD FOR **sheltered swims; beautiful views; crystal-clear water**   LOCAL GROUP **Hebridean Sea Swimmers**   LOCATION **57.8651, -6.9799**

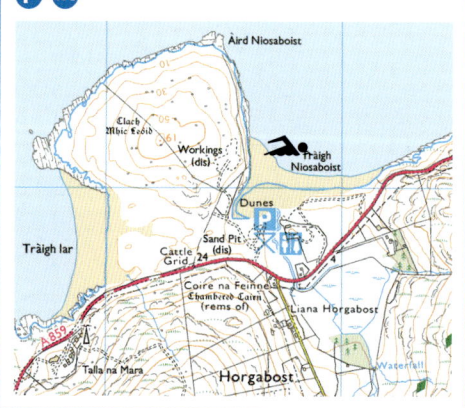

Getting there

Horgabost is just off the A859, west of Tarbert. Turn off the A859 at Horgabost Campsite. There is some parking before you enter the campsite, but for the beach, continue over the cattle grid and drive the short distance to the small beach car park right next to the sand. Please park in the designated area and respect any protected areas of machair.

There are no facilities by the beach, but there are toilets, a shop and a food truck at the campsite.

Notes

There are lots more stunning beaches to the south of Horgabost along the Harris coast, but they tend to be exposed to big swell and strong tidal currents so, as a rule, they are not suitable for swimming.

Refreshments

» **Blas bhon Iar**, Horgabost Campsite. Food truck at the campsite serving delicious soup, hot filled rolls, cake, and hot and cold drinks. Opening hours vary – check before you travel.
» **An Traigh**, Na H-Eileanan An Iar. Cafe, bar and restaurant at Talla na Mara (meaning 'Centre by the Sea') opposite Niosaboist Beach, with views across the Sound of Taransay. More of a place for meals than just hot drinks. Seasonal.
» **The Temple**, Northton. My favourite cafe on Harris with incredible food and drink incorporating local produce and Harris botanicals. Also, they are the most westerly micro coffee roasters in the UK, so good coffee is guaranteed. Seasonal.
» **Croft 36**, Northton. Lovely little shed shop with home baking, including sweet and savoury pastries.

Luskentyre Beach, Harris

No visit to Harris is complete without a visit to Luskentyre. The beach's northern section, also known as Tràigh Rosamol, is a spectacular place to swim. With miles of shell-rich sands, and views of the dark Harris hills and across to Taransay, Luskentyre often features in lists of the best beaches in the UK and worldwide.

It can get busy here on sunny days, but the beach is enormous, and I've never found it too crowded. I've enjoyed some blissful summer swims here, as well as more atmospheric splashes in the waves in the winter. Even when the clouds are grey and the rain is pouring, the beach and its vast estuary have a majestic beauty that is hard to beat.

THE SWIM

If it's not too windy and the water is calm, you can get in anywhere along the beach, although stick to the northern section (Tràigh Rosamol) rather than heading towards the estuary, where there can be sinking sands.

The entry is sandy and gently sloping. The colour of the water is incredible, and there are often silvery schools of tiny fish to spot, so make sure you wear goggles.

If there are stronger winds, I tend to head up to the far eastern end of the beach, where some rocky inlets can give a bit of shelter when changing. One winter, I changed by the rocks and found a mini freshwater waterfall to shower off under after my swim.

The sands of Tràigh Rosamol stretch for around a kilometre, so longer swims parallel to the shore are possible if conditions allow. Stick close to the beach, as there can be strong tidal currents between the beach and Taransay.

TECHNICAL INFORMATION

DESCRIPTION **beach** ORIENTATION **north-west**
TIDES **can swim at any time** ACCESS **250m walk
on a sandy path through the dunes** ENTRY **sand**
GOOD FOR **stunning scenery; turquoise water;
longer swims** LOCAL GROUP **Hebridean Sea
Swimmers** LOCATION **57.8932, -6.9558**

P **WC**

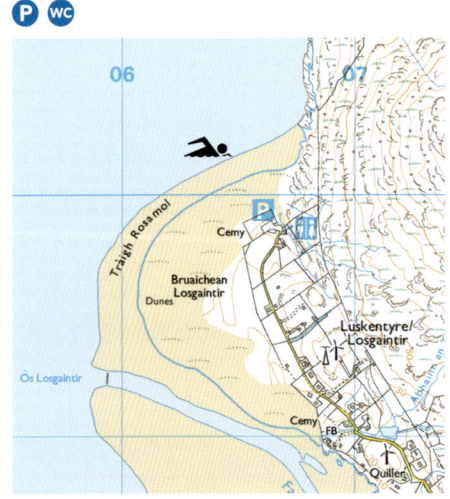

Getting there

Luskentyre is well signed (as *Losgaintir*) off the
A859, west of Tarbert. Follow the minor road for
4.5 kilometres until you reach a car park at the
northern end of the beach, where there are two
parking areas and some toilets.

Refreshments

» **The Cake Shed**, Luskentyre village. An
honesty shed with a delicious selection of
home baking and ground coffee. Amazing
ginger loaf! Make sure you have change
as it is cash only. Seasonal.

» **Luskentyre Beach Hut**, Luskentyre village.
Cute little beach hut selling hot and cold
drinks, ice creams and gifts. Seasonal.

If these are shut when you visit, head back
to Tarbert or check out the suggestions for
Horgabost Beach (see previous page), as they
are not too far away.

Reef Beach, Lewis

Reef Beach (Tràigh na Beirigh) is my favourite place to swim on Lewis. I have done lots of swimming and kayaking around the Loch Roag area and spent many nights moored alongside this sheltered beach in our live-aboard expedition boat when the weather has been too rough to travel further down the coast.

This is an incredible location for long swims parallel to the shore. The beach is 1.4 kilometres from one end to the other, and I've swum the whole length (and back) a few times. Once I was accompanied for an entire length by a curious seal, and once I nearly swam into a lion's mane jellyfish. Luckily my swim buddy spotted it before I collided with its lengthy tentacles!

THE SWIM

You can get in anywhere along the sand. The beach is generally sheltered from the worst of the Atlantic swell; it has a gently sloping entry and crystal-clear water. Several islands protect the beach, including the islands of Pabaigh Mòr and Bhàcsaigh to the north.

It is best to swim around slack tide and to stick close to shore as there can be strong tidal currents between the islands, especially at mid tide.

It may seem tempting to swim across to one of the closer islands opposite the beach. Please do not attempt this unless you have a safety kayak or paddleboard, or are swimming with someone local and knowledgeable. In my experience, islands always look much closer than they are, and people often panic when they realise how far they have to swim back again. It is not worth the risk of getting cold or battling against a quickening tide.

TECHNICAL INFORMATION

DESCRIPTION **beach** ORIENTATION **north** TIDES **can swim close to the beach at any time; best at slack tide** ACCESS **short walk along track to the beach; stony slope to get on to the main part of the beach** ENTRY **sandy; gently sloping** GOOD FOR **quick dips or long swims parallel to the shore** LOCAL GROUP **Hebridean Sea Swimmers** LOCATION **58.2190, -6.9370**

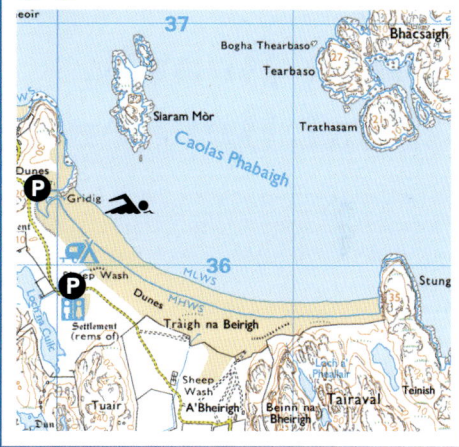

Getting there

Take the B8011 to Meavaig, then take the minor road heading north (crossing a bridge and following signs for *Riof/Reef*). At one point, it is signed in both directions as the road loops around the headland. The main parking is at the western end of the beach. There isn't a car park, but parking is allowed on designated areas of the machair. One such spot is opposite the gate where the track leads down to the beach. Please do not park in non-designated areas as the machair must be protected.

Public toilets (and additional parking) are available at the nearby campsite.

Refreshments

» **The Edge Cafe**, Aird Uig. My favourite little cafe on Lewis. Tucked out of the way in a fantastic location. You can combine a trip here with a walk to the rugged headland and shopping for local crafts in the Apex Arts and Crafts centre. Food is all freshly made by Fiona with love and care. Seasonal.

» **Uig Cafe**, Uig Community Centre. Lovely friendly cafe serving tea, coffee and lunches – there is always a great selection of delicious-looking baking in the cake cabinet. Seasonal.

Bosta Beach, Great Bernera

The first time I arrived at Bosta Beach (*Traigh Bhostaidh*) was by kayak, after an extremely windy paddle across part of Loch Roag. I will never forget the relief of turning the corner and seeing the flat calm sea and turquoise water in this gorgeous bay, which is beautifully protected from the south and west (unlike the channel I had just paddled from).

I've now been back many times, via boat and road, and still love swimming from this beach with its golden sands and views out over the smaller islands to the north-west. Mounted on the rocks at the eastern side of the beach is an unusual Time and Tide Bell – an artistic installation which rings at high tide. The bell, installed in 2010, is one of only eight bells like this in the UK.

Behind the beach is a fascinating archaeological site – a reconstruction of an Iron Age house, which was part of a Pictish village which was occupied around AD 400–800. The settlement was discovered after a ferocious storm in 1992 uncovered ancient stonework in the dunes. Remains of a Viking house were also found at the site, from which the name *Bostadh* (meaning 'Farm' in Old Norse) is thought to have derived.

THE SWIM

I tend to swim from the larger section of the beach. It's around 150 metres across, and you can easily swim parallel to the shore.

Avoid swimming out into deeper water on the eastern side of the bay. There is a very narrow channel between Great and Little Bernera which can have a strong tidal current flowing through it at certain times. I've kayaked through here when the water has been flowing fast, and I certainly wouldn't want to be caught out here by the currents if I was swimming.

If you dip in the section by the Time and Tide Bell, make sure you don't go any further out than the bell as there can be a pull from the current around the corner.

TECHNICAL INFORMATION

DESCRIPTION **beach**   ORIENTATION **north-west**
TIDES **can swim close to the beach anytime, but best at slack tide; strong tidal currents possible to the east of the beach**   ACCESS **250m walk on path through the dunes to beach**   ENTRY **sand GOOD**   FOR **sheltered swims; turquoise water; beautiful views**   LOCAL GROUP **Hebridean Sea Swimmers**   LOCATION **58.2575, -6.8833**   AVOID **east of 58.2591, -6.8819 and the channel between Great Bernera and Little Bernera**

1 Bosta Beach 2 Summer flowers at Bosta 3 Rachel swimming back to the boat at Bosta

Getting there

Great Bernera can be reached via a bridge from Lewis – follow the B8011 and the B8059. Cross the bridge and continue for seven kilometres, following brown signs towards *Bosta Beach*. At the end of the road there is a parking area with bins and public toilets.

Notes

For something more organised, Immerse Hebrides run introductory sessions and group social swims throughout the year at different locations around Lewis and Harris. There is a charge for safety cover and wetsuits can be hired at extra cost.

Refreshments

This is a lovely place to spend some time, so take a flask and a post-swim picnic and enjoy the beach and views. There are also a couple of cafe options if you want something extra.

» **Bernera Cafe**, Bernera Community Centre, Great Bernera. Not the prettiest building, but this great little community cafe serves soup, snacks, hot drinks and cakes. Limited opening hours – check before you travel.

» **Calanais Visitor Centre Cafe**, Calanais, Lewis. A fair drive away, but not far once you get back to the B8011. This handy cafe always has yummy cakes and good hot chocolate. It can get a bit busy if there are lots of visitors to the standing stones. Seasonal.

NORTH-WEST MAINLAND

Opposite Loch Maree © Calum Maclean

Sand Beach, Applecross

If you are lucky enough to visit Sand Beach on a clear day, you will be rewarded with spectacular views across the Inner Sound to the islands of Raasay, Skye and Rona. The beach is backed by massive sand dunes – one reaching over 20 metres high – and has been used for improvised avalanche training by the local mountain rescue team. You can try running up and sliding down it if you need some pre- or post-swim entertainment!

THE SWIM

From the car park, follow the road until you see the track on the left and then follow it down to the beach. You can walk across the sand at low tide until you get to the water. You may have to cross a couple of streams to get there, so wear suitable footwear.

The entry is sandy and gently sloping; it eventually gets deep enough to swim. If you get there at mid-to-high tide, I suggest walking along the grassy edge to the small building and then heading down the rocks to the water. Be careful, the rocks can be a bit seaweedy and slippery. You can also do this at low tide if you prefer. The building provides some shelter from the wind when changing.

TECHNICAL INFORMATION

DESCRIPTION **beach** ORIENTATION **west**
TIDES **can swim at any time but easier access at low tide; rocky access down to the water at high tide** ACCESS **400m to beach on a track and another 350m across sand (at low tide) or along grass (at high tide)** ENTRY **sand; shallow for a long way out** GOOD FOR **paddling; beautiful views; sunset swims** LOCATION **57.4690, -5.8682**

Getting there

Sand Beach is around eight kilometres north of Applecross village. There is a small car park at the northern end of the beach. Applecross is not the easiest place to get to, either via the northern coastal road from Shieldaig or over the infamous mountain pass from near Ardarroch. Bealach na Bà (meaning 'Pass of the Cattle') is very steep and winding and not for the faint-hearted – it is certainly a road you will never forget!

Refreshments

» **Applecross Walled Garden**, Applecross. Beautiful gardens, cafe, restaurant and gift shop. Great coffee and cake. Bookings essential. Seasonal.
» **Applecross Inn**, Applecross. Cosy pub in the village. Good food and tasty hot chocolate. Busy in the summer.

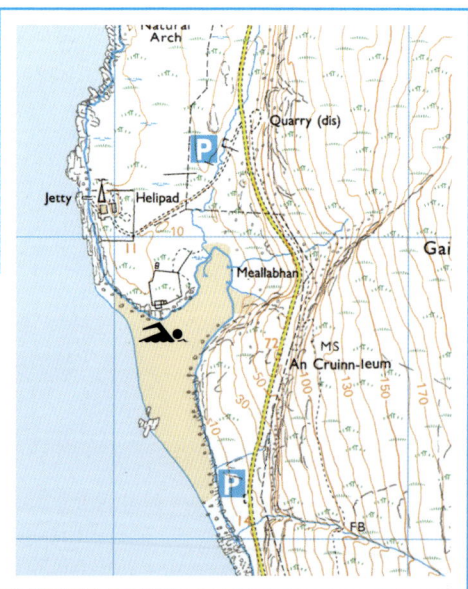

1 Exploring the seaweedy rocks near Eilean Chasgaig **2** Eilean Chasgaig

Upper Loch Torridon

I've swum in various spots while staying in Torridon village, and this has got to be my favourite place to get in. Swimming across to Eilean Chasgaig and looking over towards Beinn Alligin ('Jewelled Mountain' in Gaelic), this has to be one of the best water-level views in the Highlands.

The variety of wildlife in and around Upper Loch Torridon is amazing. Look out for otters, seals and porpoises in the water and golden eagles soaring high overhead. I've even been lucky enough to see a white-tailed eagle while swimming here. Dip your eyes beneath the surface and you get a chance to discover this fascinating underwater world – seaweed, starfish, delicate dahlia anemones on the rocks, and mussels growing in thick clusters under buoys. Make sure you take your goggles.

THE SWIM

It is only possible to swim here around high tide. At low tide, there is no water. At high tide, you can enter the water from the shingle by the grass, and it's less than 150 metres over to the main island. At mid tide, you can continue along the fence line and get in from the rocks overlooking the island. Be careful, as it can be slippery.

TECHNICAL INFORMATION

DESCRIPTION **sea loch** ORIENTATION **north-west** TIDES **only possible around high tide (no water at low tide)** ACCESS **600m walk on good track; stile to beach** ENTRY **shingle** GOOD FOR **swims to the island; spectacular views of the mountains; wildlife spotting** LOCATION **57.5300, -5.5355** AVOID **if you don't like seaweed**

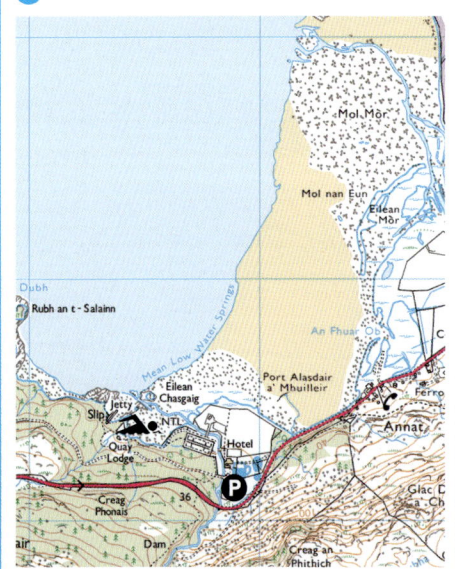

Getting there

Head to the eastern end of Upper Loch Torridon on the A896. Park near the Torridon Hotel, either in one of the lay-bys (there are a few near the hotel) or in the small car park adjacent to the hotel (signposted *Bo & Muc Restaurant* and *The Beinn Bar*).

Access

From the car park, head towards the bike hire building, through the courtyard behind Bo & Muc Restaurant and follow the track over a small bridge. There is a sign after the bridge – ignore the paths marked on this sign. Instead, follow the tarmac round to the right and then take the next left, following the path as it skirts the hotel's kitchen garden. After a couple of hundred metres, the path emerges at the shore. Climb over the little wooden stile on to a grassy area overlooking the loch.

Notes

There is often lots of seaweed in this part of the loch, so it's not for those who don't like it. I find the seaweed fascinating and lovely to look at underwater, but I know some people wouldn't like being tickled!

Refreshments

» **Beinn Bar**, Torridon Hotel, Achnasheen. Next to Bo & Muc Restaurant, this bar is sometimes open to non-residents (check before travelling) for tea, coffee and cakes.

» **Wee Whistle Stop Cafe**, Loch Torridon Community Centre, Torridon. Fabulous cafe with great home-baked cakes, traybakes and scones. Wide selection of light bites and sandwiches available and plenty of vegan options too.

1 Loch Clair with Beinn Eighe and Liathach behind © Shutterstock/Joe Dunckley

Loch Clair

Swimming in Loch Clair is a magical experience. The views of Beinn Eighe and Liathach from across the water are some of the finest mountain views I've seen while swimming. Even when shrouded in cloud, the looming Munros are an impressive sight. The reflections are superb if you are lucky enough to visit on a calm day. The first time I swam here, I only managed a quick dip between heavy rain showers, watching the weather move through the glen. Since then, I've stopped to swim here every time I pass. It's only a ten-minute walk from the road, but you feel like you are a million miles away from the hustle and bustle of the world.

THE SWIM

The entry is quite gravelly and rocky underfoot, turning a bit weedy and soft as you get deeper, so make sure you have something on your feet. It isn't long before it becomes deep enough to swim, and the views are sublime. As well as towering Beinn Eighe to the north, at this entry point Sgùrr Dubh is straight ahead of you and the mighty Munro Liathach is behind and to the right.

Please note that this is a fishing loch, and the owners of the houses at the southern end of the loch are not always welcoming to swimmers. It's best to keep up towards the road end of the loch. If you see a fishing boat on the loch, please make sure you keep a good distance away. This is a loch more suited to dipping and soaking up the views, rather than longer swims along the length of the loch.

TECHNICAL INFORMATION

DESCRIPTION **freshwater loch**   MAXIMUM DEPTH
30m   LENGTH **1.7km**   MAXIMUM WIDTH **500m**
ELEVATION **100m**   ACCESS **800m walk on a
good track; fairly flat**   ENTRY **rocky/gravelly**
GOOD FOR **spectacular mountain views; quick dips**
LOCATION **57.5629, -5.3428**   AVOID **southern
end of the loch and fishing boats**

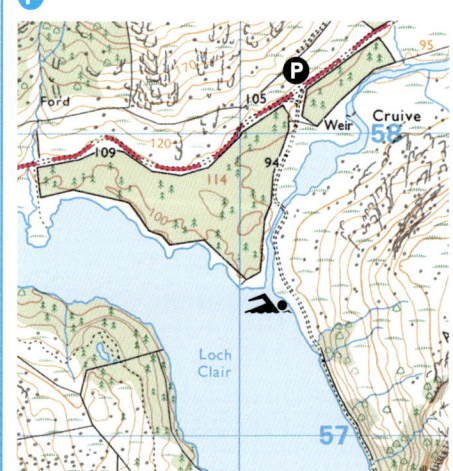

Getting there

Loch Clair is accessed from the A896 between
Kinlochewe and Torridon village. There is a
small parking area, more like an enlarged lay-by,
with space for about six cars opposite the turn
off for the private road to Coulin Lodge. If the
parking is full, come back another time. Do not
block the estate road – it is narrow, and access
is required at all times.

Access

From the car park, cross the road and follow
the track opposite, signposted *Coulin Estate,
footpath only*. Continue past the cattle grid,
go through a gate and cross a wooden bridge.
Continue on until you reach the point where the
river exits the loch. Shortly past this, there is a

lay-by on the left; just opposite the lay-by is a
small track that takes you up to a little viewpoint
over the loch. You'll see the rocky and gravelly
beach below.

Refreshments

» **Kinlochewe Service Station** is the closest
option if you're travelling north. It's nothing
fancy, but there is a great little cafe
attached to the fuel station – a perfect stop
for some post-swim grub. Good coffee,
delicious cakes and great toasties.
» **Wee Whistle Stop Cafe**, Loch Torridon
Community Centre, Torridon. (See page 60.)

Loch Maree

Loch Maree is a magical place to swim, with
spectacular views and gorgeous clean, dark
water.

It is the largest freshwater loch in the
North West Highlands (the fourth largest in
Scotland) and is famous for its history, islands
and remnants of ancient Caledonian pine
forest. There are five large, wooded islands
and over 60 smaller ones, all with international
importance for their special wildlife and
biodiversity.

BEINN EIGHE NATIONAL NATURE RESERVE

This was the first place I ever swam in Loch Maree,
and I still remember the incredible sight of the
mighty Munro, Slioch, dusted with an icing-
sugar-like layer of snow, towering before me.

It is easy to access the loch from the car
park just down from the information building.
The entry is pebbly and stony, so protective
footwear is essential. In winter I've changed
under the green roof of the information building.
I don't suppose this would be possible when it
is busy in the summer, but it provided a useful
shelter from the wind and rain at the time.

Another option is to keep walking along the path (heading west), over a small burn and slightly further along the bay to a pebbly beach, which is a bit more private. It is still relatively close to the road, but more hidden and sheltered.

SLATTADALE

This tucked-away swimming spot offers easy access to the loch (from right next to the car park) and spectacular views of the hills beyond.

The entry here is gravelly and drops off quite quickly into deep water. Once you are in, potter around and soak up the spectacular views, or head off for a longer swim, parallel to the shore, or out towards the islands.

Being close to the islands, this is a popular launching spot for canoes. It's just over a kilometre to the wee beach on the western side of Eilean Ruairidh Mòr, the closest decent-sized island. While only non-motorised crafts are allowed on the loch, make sure you use a tow float, especially if you plan a longer swim.

Please note that rare black-throated divers nest on the islands between April and September and are specially protected by law. Read the signage in the car park and keep your distance to avoid disturbance.

TECHNICAL INFORMATION

DESCRIPTION **freshwater loch** MAXIMUM DEPTH **110m** LENGTH **20km** MAXIMUM WIDTH **3.5km** ELEVATION **10m** ACCESS **swim entry close to car parks** ENTRY **gravelly/stony** GOOD FOR **stunning scenery; quick dips; long swims towards the islands** LOCATION **Beinn Eighe National Nature Reserve 57.6314, -5.3492; Slattadale 57.6899, -5.5434**

Beinn Eighe National Nature Reserve

Slattadale

Getting there – Loch Maree

Loch Maree lies on the A832, to the north of Kinlochewe.

Access – Beinn Eighe National Nature Reserve

The car park (which is around four kilometres north of Kinlochewe) is well signed from the A832. Both swimming spots are a short walk from the car park.

Access – Slattadale

From Kinlochewe, head north on the A832 for 18 kilometres. The turning to the car park is quite easy to miss (the sign for the turning is tiny) – it is around 200 metres after the green *Slattadale* sign. Follow the narrow road, which then turns into a bumpy track. Keep going to reach a large parking area with picnic benches. There is a toilet block (seasonal) by the car park. The swim entry is right next to the car park.

Refreshments

The Beinn Eighe swimming spot has picnic benches if you want to bring your own supplies. Alternatively, it is also a short drive from Kinlochewe if you need something hot to warm you up after your dip.

 » **Kinlochewe Service Station**, Kinlochewe. (See page 62.)

For Slattadale, there isn't anything nearby, but there are picnic benches so bring your own post-swim food and drinks, or head north to Gairloch (see the recommendations for Gaineamh Mhòr opposite).

Gaineamh Mhòr, Gairloch

Just south of the village of Gairloch, Gaineamh Mhòr is a beautiful, sheltered sandy beach backed by dunes. Also known locally as Golf Course Beach, Gaineamh Mhòr translates to 'Big Sand' in Gaelic and, at low tide, it is clear why – a vast expanse of sand is revealed, adding an extra 150 metres to your walk down to the sea.

I've enjoyed some wonderful swims here, especially in winter. The sand rippling beneath my feet, strewn with fragments of shell, and oystercatchers swooping over the water as I swim. At the southern end of the bay, by the rocks of the An Dùn headland, the water is often calm and turquoise, even when the waves crash at the northern end of the beach.

THE SWIM

You can swim anywhere along the beach. Swimming at high-to-mid tide is preferable, but only to avoid the long walk down to the water, which can be chilly if it is windy. If it is a bit wavy, the southern end of the beach tends to be a bit more sheltered, especially at mid-to-high tide, as the rocky headland protects it. The bay is about 500 metres across if you want to do a longer swim.

1 & 2 Loch Maree © Bernie McGee   **3** Gaineamh Mhòr, Gairloch © Richard Elliott

TECHNICAL INFORMATION

DESCRIPTION **beach**   ORIENTATION **west**
TIDES **best at high-to-mid tide, but possible at
any time**   ACCESS **short walk to the beach on
a wooden walkway**   ENTRY **sand**   GOOD FOR
longer swims; winter dips; sunsets   LOCAL GROUP
Gairloch Dippers   SEPA BATHING WATERS **water
quality tested June–September**   LOCATION
57.7161, -5.6879

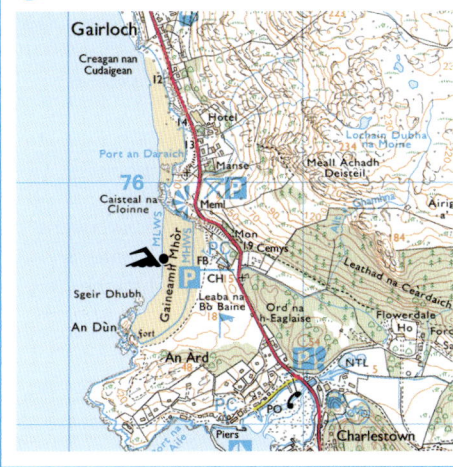

Getting there

The beach is south of Gairloch village and is
easy to find, with parking directly off the A832
at Gairloch Golf Club, opposite a white church.
Access to the beach is signposted via a wooden
walkway through the dunes.

Refreshments

» **Links Cafe**, Gairloch Golf Club. Great little
 cafe right by the beach at the golf club –
 also welcomes non-golfers. Good fish and
 chips and tasty hot chocolate.
» **Coast Coffee**, Gairloch. Excellent selection
 of hot drinks and cakes. Seasonal.
» **Crumbs**, Gairloch. Great little takeaway
 offering a wide range of goodies, including
 delicious pies and naughty cakes.

3

Firemore Beach

Firemore Beach is comprised of two large bays connected by a central rocky headland. I've always found this an excellent place for swimming and wildlife watching. I've seen diving birds catching fish underwater while I've bobbed about in the waves. Other swimmers have seen eagles, dolphins and whales, and watched otters feeding on the shore.

The beach has a fascinating history and was the location of a boom defence depot during World War II. Loch Ewe was one of the main gathering points for ships which were part of convoys that brought supplies across the Atlantic from America during the war and was heavily defended with anti-submarine nets. The depot would have stored the nets, floats and cables needed for the operation and upkeep of the boom defence. After the war ended, it was redeveloped as a marine research unit, which closed in the 1990s. It is now a quiet beach and one of my favourite west coast swimming spots.

THE SWIM

This beach has a gently sloping, sandy entry into stunningly clear water. It is divided into two bays, the larger northern section (where I usually swim) being just under 400 metres across and the smaller southern section being around 300 metres to the rocks.

A small group of local swimmers meet at Firemore Beach every Sunday afternoon – I bumped into them (by chance) last time I was swimming here. If you are keen for a double dip, the Ewe Wild Swimmers' weekly, Sunday morning swim is at Boom Beach at Mellon Charles (on the other side of Loch Ewe).

TECHNICAL INFORMATION

DESCRIPTION **beach**   ORIENTATION **north-east**
TIDES **can swim at any time**   ACCESS **short walk
to the beach on a solid track**   ENTRY **sand**
GOOD FOR **swims along the bays; wildlife
watching**   LOCAL GROUP **Ewe Wild Swimmers**
LOCATION **57.8323, -5.6764; 57.8337, -5.6806**

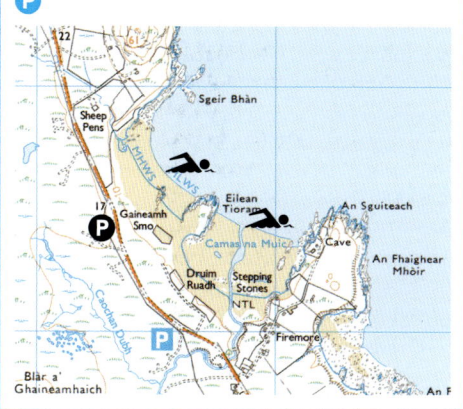

Getting there

Firemore Beach lies on the western shore
of Loch Ewe. Take the A832 to the village of
Poolewe, at the southern tip of Loch Ewe.
Turn off the A832 in the village on to the B8057,
signposted *Inverasdale & Cove*. Follow the
road for 10 kilometres to reach the beach on
the right. There is a lay-by on the right and,
a little further along, a small car park on the left,
with room for around six or eight cars. Tracks
run from both parking options to the beach.

Refreshments

» **The Old Schoolhouse Tearoom**, Inverasdale. Recently renovated community cafe
less than two kilometres down the road
from the beach. Home-made cakes, teas
and coffees. Limited opening times, check
before you travel.
» **Bridge Cottage Cafe & Sourdough
Bakery**, Poolewe. Lovely small cafe
serving delicious home-made cakes and
bread. Tasty meals, locally roasted coffee
and great luxury spiced lattes and hot
chocolate.
» **Coffee and Bakes**, Poolewe. Small
takeaway cabin with some outdoor seating.
Excellent selection of cakes and savoury
flapjacks (including some good gluten-free
options). Great hot chocolate. Seasonal.

Mellon Udrigle

With clear turquoise water, clean white sand and
spectacular mountain views across Gruinard Bay,
Mellon Udrigle is one of my favourite places
to swim on the west coast of Scotland. To the
north-east, the views include the distinctive
profile of Suilven near Lochinver, while to the
south-east, the views conclude with a glimpse
of An Teallach.

I am lucky enough to have friends who live
just up the road in Laide, and this has always
been a great, sheltered spot to swim when
I have visited, even in the middle of winter.

THE SWIM

It is a nice, gently sloping entry to the water.
I have had some magical swims here, marvelling at the colour of the water (goggles recommended), gazing at the incredible views,
floating on my back and watching the moon
rise over the mountains. If you want to swim
up and down the beach, the bay is around
250 metres across.

1 Mellon Udrigle beach © David Weekes **2** Fiona getting ready for a winter dip at Mellon Udrigle

TECHNICAL INFORMATION

DESCRIPTION **beach** ORIENTATION **north-east**
TIDES **can swim at any time** ACCESS **short walk
to the beach** ENTRY **sand** GOOD FOR **short
dips or longer swims around the bay; seal
spotting** LOCAL GROUP **Ewe Wild Swimmers**
LOCATION **57.9020, -5.5569**

Getting there
Mellon Udrigle is on the Rubha Mòr peninsula,
west of Ullapool. Take the A832 to the village
of Laide, then take the single-track coastal road
heading north for around five kilometres until
you reach a small car park on your right. Parking
is limited, and there isn't much space for large
vehicles. There is also a campsite adjacent to
the beach, but there are no facilities for day
visitors, so make sure you bring everything that
you need with you.

Access
From the car park, it is an easy 100-metre walk
along a boardwalk to the beach. There are a
couple of streams to cross, which can be pretty
dark and peaty, with lots of seaweed washed up
at this end of the bay. Walk a bit further and you
will find pristine sand and a remarkably clean
beach. The dunes can provide some shelter
from the wind when changing.

Refreshments
» **Oran-na-Mara Cafe**, Aultbea. Cosy cafe
  and gift shop. Good cakes and yummy
  lunch.
» **Aroma Cafe**, The Perfume Studio, Mellon
  Charles. Great views, home-made bread,
  soup, scones and cakes. Seasonal.

Achnahaird Beach

Achnahaird Beach is a vast expanse of sand tucked into a granite-lined inlet on the remote Coigach peninsula, to the north-west of Ullapool. With spectacular views over the imposing mountains of Assynt, this north-facing beach can be pretty exposed in the winter, but it is often sheltered in the spring and summer months. If you catch it on a calm day, you will be rewarded with crystal-clear water and perfect swimming conditions.

THE SWIM

This beach looks quite different at high and low tides. My preference is to swim here at mid-to-low tide, when the water is falling. At high tide, the water is so shallow, and you'll end up doing a lot of paddling in ankle-deep water. At mid-to-low tide, the entry is sandy and gently sloping. It still takes a while to get deep enough to swim but, once you are in, the water can be stunningly clear, and it is a perfect place for gentle swims and soaking up the views above and below the water.

It is around 200 metres across the bay, swimming parallel to the shore. On calm days it is possible to swim from the beach back to the car park (or vice versa), along the rocky, western side of the bay. When I have swum from the beach car park, it has been around 400 metres to the beach (one way), but obviously, this depends on the level of the tide at the time. Ensure you have something to protect your feet if you get out along the rocks, as they can be slippery and sharp in places.

The tide rises quickly here, so make sure you leave your kit somewhere it won't get wet when the tide rises.

TECHNICAL INFORMATION

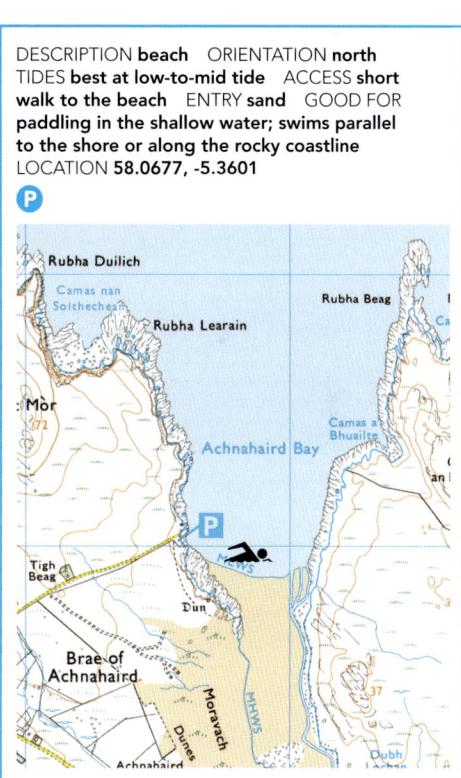

DESCRIPTION **beach**   ORIENTATION **north**
TIDES **best at low-to-mid tide**   ACCESS **short walk to the beach**   ENTRY **sand**   GOOD FOR **paddling in the shallow water; swims parallel to the shore or along the rocky coastline**
LOCATION **58.0677, -5.3601**

Getting there

Achnahaird Beach is on the northern coast of the Coigach peninsula, north-west of Ullapool. Take the A835 north from Ullapool then turn on to a small single-track road at Drumrunie, signposted *Achiltibuie*. Watch out for sheep (and occasionally cows) on the road. Turn right after around 19 kilometres, following the signpost towards *Achnahaird*. When you get to the main village, follow signposts to the *Beach* to reach the car park. Parking is free; there are no facilities (apart from some bins). While the car park can

get busy with camper vans in the summer, it is generally quieter than other beaches along this section of coastline as it is a bit of a detour off the popular North Coast 500 route.

Access

From the car park, it is a five-to-ten-minute walk down to the beach. The track is solid at first, then slopes down over the grass to the beach. At low tide, it can then be another 150 or 200 metres further across the sand until you get to the water.

Refreshments

This is a remote beach with not many eating options close by. Ideally, stock up on snacks in Ullapool and bring a post-swim picnic.

» **Am Fuaran Bar**, Altandhu. If you need hot food, this is the best nearby option at around five kilometres from the beach. Fantastic seafood, hearty pub grub and open for lunch and dinner all year round. There is even another little beach opposite the bar that you can walk down to via the campsite if you are up for a double dip.

Achmelvich

The beaches at Achmelvich have spectacular white sand and mesmerisingly clear water in shades of aquamarine and bright blue. My last swim here was on a grey, windy day, but the water was still astonishingly turquoise and inviting for a play in the waves.

Along with the main beach, there is also a second beach to the north, known locally as Vestey's Beach. When Achmelvich Beach gets busy, this beach is usually quieter. Vestey's Beach faces west and can subsequently be a bit more exposed, but it is possible to swim between the two on very calm days.

THE SWIM

You can get in anywhere along the sand on Achmelvich Beach. It is a gently sloping entry and great for paddling and playing in the waves. Make sure you bring goggles to fully experience the spectacular turquoise water. When the area is busy, watch out for boats that tend to moor up towards the southern end of the bay.

You can swim north around the rocky headland to Vestey's Beach if it is exceptionally calm. This is around 500 metres (each way), and you must watch out for submerged rocks. In good conditions, there are likely to be other water users around, so tow floats are essential.

If you plan to swim from Vestey's Beach, it also has a gently sloping entry and you can get in anywhere you fancy along the beach. There is a 100-metre-long sandy-bottomed channel between the headland and some rocks close to Vestey's Beach which is lovely to swim through if conditions allow.

TECHNICAL INFORMATION

DESCRIPTION **beach**   ORIENTATION **north-west; west**   TIDES **can swim at any time**   ACCESS **short walk to Achmelvich Beach; 500m walk to Vestey's Beach**   ENTRY **sand**   GOOD FOR **paddling; swims along the rocky coastline; sunset dips**   SEPA BATHING WATERS **water quality tested June–September (Achmelvich Beach)**   LOCATION **Achmelvich Beach 58.1700, -5.3067; Vestey's Beach 58.1730, -5.3032**

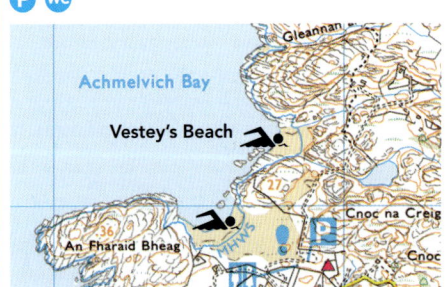

Getting there

Achmelvich is well signed from Lochinver. Head north out of Lochinver on the A837 then turn on to the B869. After two kilometres, take the single-track road on the left. Follow this road past a campsite, and you will see a small sign directing you to the *Beach Car Park* on your right. The car park can get very busy in summer. At the time of writing the car park is free to use, but there are plans to expand the car park and introduce parking charges. There are toilets (seasonal) and a ranger on site in the summer.

As the beach is only seven kilometres from Lochinver, it is possible to walk or cycle to the beach (this can be a good option in high season, when the car park is likely to be busy).

Access

Achmelvich Beach is an easy, 200-metre walk from the car park, following a sandy path through the dunes.

Vestey's Beach is slightly trickier to get to on foot. Follow the large track that heads north out of the car park (no vehicle access) signposted *Alltan' abradhan*. Where the main track bears right, turn left on to a smaller sandy path which crosses a stream and drops steeply over rocks to the beach. Alternatively, take the longer, gentler route, which sticks to the main track until it forks. At this point, head left over the grass, following the slope and stream down to Vestey's Beach.

Refreshments

» **Tidal Gifts and The Hatch**, Achmelvich. Currently the only coffee shop and daytime food and drink option in Achmelvich. Tea, coffee, ice cream and tasty traybakes. Seasonal.
» **Shore Chip Shop**, Shore Caravan Site, Achmelvich. Excellent fish and chips, right by the beach. Seasonal and limited opening hours (evenings only) – check before you travel.
» **Flossie's Beach Store**, Clachtoll. A little blue shed shop in Clachtoll, where there is another lovely beach. Great coffee, yummy hot food and a basic shop for the community and nearby campsite. Open all year round.
» **Lochinver Larder**, Lochinver. If you like pies, then this place is for you. Eat in or pick up a couple of pies on your way to the beach for a tasty post-swim pie picnic. Meat, fish, vegetarian and sweet pies are available.

1

2

N

0   15 kilometres

① Durness
② Tongue
Thurso
John o' Groats
A836
A897
A838
A836
Kinbrace
A882
A9
A99
Helmsdale
A9
⑦

Orkney Islands
Stromness
③ A964 ④ Kirkwall
Hoy
A961
Stroma
South Ronaldsay

Shetland Islands
Unst
Haroldswick ⑥
North Roe
A968
Yell
Fetla
Hillswick
Sandness
A970
Whalsay
Lerwick
Scalloway
Bressay
West Burra
⑤ Hoswick
Grutness

FAR NORTH

Opposite Skaw Beach, Unst, Shetland © Brian Stallwood

Balnakeil Beach, Durness

Close to the extreme north-western tip of mainland Scotland, Balnakeil Beach is an exceptional crescent of white sand backed by massive sand dunes to the east. The beach forms one side of a narrow peninsula that stretches out to the rocky headland of Faraid Head. It is a spectacular place to play in the waves or enjoy a long, leisurely swim parallel to the shore. While the beach is west facing, it is beautifully protected to the south and west by the Cape Wrath landmass, making it surprisingly sheltered from the prevailing winds.

Balnakeil (*Baile na Cille*) comes from the Gaelic for 'Farm' or 'Settlement of the Church'. The area's links to Christianity date back to the eighth century (possibly even before), and the beach is also still part of a working farm. It is not unusual for there to be a herd of cows on the beach – don't worry though, with several kilometres of sand, there is plenty of space for everyone!

THE SWIM

You can get into the water anywhere along the sand, but I would walk at least a hundred metres or so along the beach to avoid rocks at the southern end of the beach and the streams and debris (such as seaweed) that tend to wash up in this area.

Ideally, swims should be planned around high tide, as otherwise it can be a good 250-metre walk out to the water. This isn't so bad on warm, sunny days, but not so fun when it is cold and windy. The entry is gently sloping, and it is easy to stay in relatively shallow water if you want to.

Once you are in, you can bob about in the waves or set off for a longer swim parallel to the shore. The first stretch of beach is around 750 metres long. If you are swimming at high tide, be aware that there are some submerged rocks directly in front of the first headland.

1 & 2 Balnakeil Beach © Brian Stallwood

TECHNICAL INFORMATION

DESCRIPTION **beach**   ORIENTATION **west**
TIDES **best at high tide**   ACCESS **short walk from
the car park**   ENTRY **sand**   GOOD FOR **playing
in the waves; long swims parallel to the shore**
LOCATION **58.5774, -4.7678**

Getting there

To get to Balnakeil, take the minor road running
west out of Durness, signposted *Golf Course*
and *Balnakeil Craft Village*. There is a small car
park by the church. This can get busy as it is a
popular stop on the North Coast 500. However,
if you carry on along the minor road, round
the walls of the cemetery, you'll get to the golf
course car park (strictly no overnight parking),
where there is some more space. Then you just
have to walk for a few minutes back along the
road to access the beach.

If you are staying in Durness, it is possible
to walk two kilometres along the road from the
village to the beach. You can also catch a bus
from Durness, which will drop you at Balnakeil
Craft Village, a short walk from the beach.

Refreshments

» **Cocoa Mountain**, Balnakeil Craft Village.
  It is seriously worth going for a swim just
  so you can have a Cocoa Mountain hot
  chocolate! Heaven for chocoholics; other
  food is also available.
» **Meet and Eat**, Balnakeil Craft Village.
  A not-quite-so-chocolatey alternative
  to Cocoa Mountain. A great lunch stop,
  and good coffee and cake.

1 Harbour beach, Talmine Bay   **2** Talmine Bay © Shutterstock/Helen Hotson

Talmine Bay

Protected to the north by a pier that connects the mainland with Eilean Creagach, the east-facing beach at Talmine is one of my favourite spots to swim along this wild northern coastline. The bay is shallow and inviting, with crystal-clear water and wonderful views over the nearby Rabbit Islands and the hills of Brae Tongue rising against the sky on the opposite side of the Kyle of Tongue.

This is also an excellent spot for wildlife watching, with dolphins and seals regularly sighted. Make sure you scan the waves for the triangular fins of harbour porpoise, as this stretch of coastline is a favourite breeding ground for them.

3 Main beach, Talmine Bay

THE SWIM

There are two main entry points for swimming in the bay, the main beach and the smaller harbour beach. Both have sandy entries, although the main beach is a bit pebbly in places.

Tow floats are essential here, particularly if swimming anywhere near the harbour. Watch out for boats and people fishing from the rocks. Only swim from the harbour beach if the harbour is quiet, and watch out for mooring ropes.

TECHNICAL INFORMATION

DESCRIPTION **beach** ORIENTATION **east** TIDES **can swim at any time** ACCESS **park by the beach** ENTRY **sandy** GOOD FOR **short dips or longer swims around the bay; picnics on the beach** LOCATION **58.5335, -4.4268**

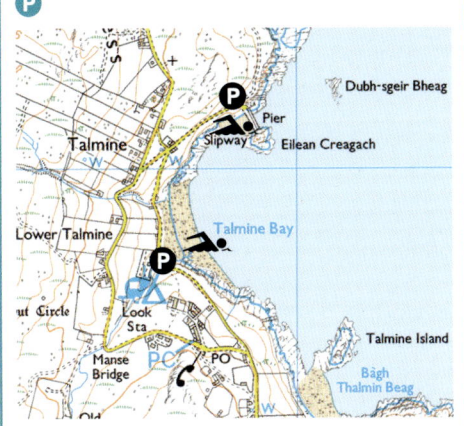

Getting there

Talmine Bay is reached by turning off the A838 on to a narrow single-track road just west of the Kyle of Tongue causeway. The minor, no-through road heading north is signposted to *Melness* and *Talmine*. Follow the road for around four kilometres until you get to where the road splits in the village of Talmine.

For the main beach, take the lower road and park at the small grassy area by the burn, which takes you directly on to the beach. There are a few picnic benches and, being grass, the parking area can get a bit soggy after rain. From here, walk up and over the pebbles to reach the beautiful sandy part of the beach.

Carry on along the road (or take the upper road) and you will find a small amount of parking near the harbour. This is unsuitable for large vehicles due to the tight turning area if other cars are already there. Overnight parking is not permitted. If you do choose to park here, make sure you don't block the track or access to the slipway.

Refreshments

» **Talmine Stores & Post Office**, Talmine. On the upper road through Talmine. Good for basic snacks and picnic supplies.

» **Weaver's Craft Shop & Cafe**, Woodend. Small cafe and gift shop between Tongue and Coldbackie. Definitely worth a stop if you are heading back on the A836 towards Thurso. Excellent hot food, drinks and cakes. The cheesecake is superb.

Ness Slipway, Orkney

I had one of my most unexpectedly glorious swims at this little slipway near the Point of Ness. After a very 'challenging' ferry crossing in stormy conditions and a misty start to the day, the sun blazed through the cloud in the afternoon, and we enjoyed sparkling water and blue skies as we floated along, gazing up at Stromness's historic skyline.

The old town sits along the water's edge, undulating with the rise and fall of the shoreline; higgledy-piggledy houses with slipways to the water's edge bringing back memories of transatlantic trading and whaling expeditions that left from this harbour in years gone by.

Ness Slipway is now a popular spot for many Orkney swimmers. Beautifully sheltered from the majority of wind directions and calm even when huge waves batter the rest of the western coastline, it is a wonderful place to watch the world go by. You might even get to wave at the people arriving on the Scrabster–Stromness ferry as it comes into the harbour – make sure you don't get in its way!

THE SWIM

Access to the water is down the concrete slipway. Be careful as it can be slippery underfoot.

Once you've entered the water, you must turn left or right and swim parallel to the shore, rather than straight out across the harbour entrance. This is a safe place to swim as long as you are sensible. Tow floats are absolutely essential for visibility.

You can swim parallel to the shore for around 500 metres or so back towards Stromness. If you swim the other way, make sure you don't swim around the headland by the campsite as there can be very strong tides at the Point of Ness.

Always bear in mind that this is a public slipway. If a boat uses the slipway, wait until it is clear before entering the water. The local sailing club uses the slipway a couple of times a week (Thursday evenings and Sunday afternoons at the time of writing) throughout the summer. Avoid swimming here during these times.

TECHNICAL INFORMATION

DESCRIPTION **harbour**   ORIENTATION **north-east**
TIDES **better at high tide (but possible at any time)**
ACCESS **easy; the slipway is right next to the road and a small car park**   ENTRY **concrete slipway; can be slippery**   GOOD FOR **sheltered swims; a pre- or post-ferry plunge**   LOCAL GROUP **Orkney Polar Bears**   LOCATION **58.9536, -3.2975**
AVOID **ferry lanes**

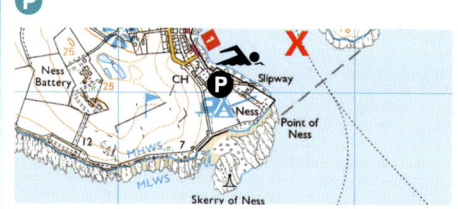

Getting there

Ness Slipway is close to the Point of Ness Campsite, around 1.5 kilometres from Stromness ferry terminal. It is nice to walk or cycle to the slipway along the harbour-side road. If you're driving, it is better to take the back road (literally called Back Road) to avoid the narrow streets. There is space to park a few cars next to the slipway.

Refreshments

» **The Bayleaf Delicatessen**, Stromness. There are plenty of options in Stromness, but this is my favourite little deli. Excellent hot chocolate and arguably the best coffee in Orkney. Also, a good selection of sweet treats (yummy brownies and cinnamon buns) and filled rolls. Takeaway only, but there are a couple of benches outside.

1 Happy Sarah at Ness Slipway   **2** Swimming up to the *MV Juniata* shipwreck, Inganess

Inganess, Orkney

Close to Kirkwall, sheltered from the worst of the weather and waves, and suitable for swimming at any stage of the tide, Inganess has become my go-to swimming spot when visiting Orkney Mainland. The beach doesn't look very inspiring when you first approach it until you see the imposing shipwreck of the *MV Juniata* looming out of the water. You can't come to Orkney without swimming out to a shipwreck.

The *MV Juniata* belonged to the fleet of sacrificial 'blockships' sunk to protect the Royal Navy fleet anchored at Scapa Flow during World War II. After the war, it was refloated for salvaging but was subsequently beached at Inganess Bay and left to rust. It is now a nesting place for Arctic terns in the late spring and summer.

I was lucky enough to join a group of Orkney Polar Bears for my first swim around the *MV Juniata*. As we swam, a small plane took off and flew directly overhead – we waved, and I swear the pilot dipped the wing of the plane and waved back!

THE SWIM

With its gently sloping, sandy entry, this beach is perfect for quick dips or a long swim around the shipwreck. If you are keen to swim around the ship but don't want to swim too far, make sure you go at low tide when you can practically walk up to the wreck. At high tide, it's a loop of approximately 500 metres around the boat. Alternatively, if you prefer swimming parallel to the shore, it is around 500 metres (one way) across the bay.

This is a regular swimming location for members of the Orkney Polar Bears. If you want some company, get in contact (via their Facebook page), as there will be Kirkwall-based folk swimming most days.

If you plan to swim around the *MV Juniata*, ensure you don't go too close to the wreck. There can be submerged rusty metal close to the ship that you might not see. Do not touch or climb up on to the wreck. In the summer, Arctic terns nesting on the boat will dive-bomb you if you swim too close. They are small birds, but they have very pointy beaks. Keep your distance so as not to disturb them.

1

2

1 Southern side, St Ninian's Beach © Alastair Goodridge   **2 St Ninian's Beach tombolo** © Alastair Goodridge

TECHNICAL INFORMATION

DESCRIPTION **beach**   ORIENTATION **north-east**
TIDES **can swim at any time; shorter distance out
to the shipwreck at low tide**   ACCESS **car park
directly opposite sandy beach**   ENTRY **sand**
GOOD FOR **swimming around the shipwreck;
handstand practice; sunrise dips**   LOCAL GROUP
Orkney Polar Bears   LOCATION **58.9625, -2.9139**

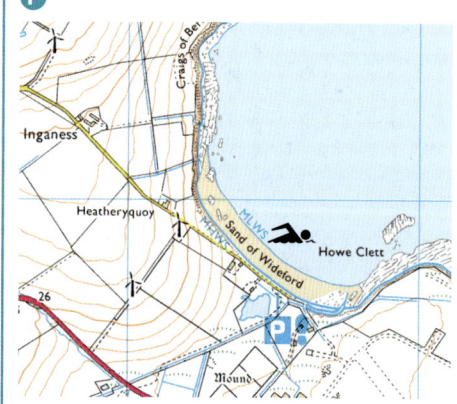

Getting there
Head south out of Kirkwall on the A960 (initially
heading towards the airport). Turn left after a
grassy triangle on to Inganess Road (signposted
to *Inganess*) and follow this road to the car park
opposite the beach. Parking is limited to around
eight cars. There is a narrow path down to the
beach opposite the car park.

Refreshments
There isn't anything on the doorstep but lots
of places in Kirkwall. Here are a couple of my
favourites.
» **The Daily Scoop**, Kirkwall. Pancakes,
waffles, hot chocolate and home bakes.
Excellent post-swim grub.
» **Cafelolz**, Kirkwall. Exceptional home-made
cakes, great coffee and yummy food made
from locally sourced, fresh produce. A real
treat for the tastebuds.

St Ninian's Beach, Shetland

The beach at St Ninian's Isle has always
been high on my list of swimming locations
to visit. Being a geography geek (it was my
undergraduate degree subject), I've always
been fascinated by coastal processes and
formations.

You'll find the largest tombolo in the UK
here; it was formed by waves from the Atlantic
being refracted and diffracted around the island
and meeting on the leeward side. In the central
zone, sand and pebbles on the sea floor have
been swept along by waves and accumulated
to form the natural sand tombolo (causeway)
connecting the island to the mainland. Only
occasionally, during high spring tides and major
storms, is the tombolo breached by waves.

Arriving here for the first time, mist hung
low over the water and waves crashed on the
northern shore. Despite this, the ribbon of sand
connecting St Ninian's Isle to the mainland
still took my breath away, and the sea on
the southern side of the beach was perfectly
sheltered and ideal for swimming. On other
days, depending on the wind direction, the
northern side is better for swimming. On one
occasion, I double dipped, playing in the waves
on one side and then doing a longer swim in
the perfectly calm water on the other side.

THE SWIM
From the road, you get a good view of the
beach and can see which side will be most
sheltered for swimming. There is a good, sandy
track heading down to the beach. You can get
into the water anywhere along the beach on the
southern side. My preferred changing area on
the southern side is round by the rocks at the

beach's eastern end, where some nice sheltered rocky outcrops offer a bit of protection from the often-fierce wind.

If you want to do a longer swim parallel with the shore, the southern side is slightly longer at around 600 metres (one way). On the northern side, you can swim for roughly 450 metres parallel to the shore but make sure you avoid the area closest to the road (the eastern end of the beach), as there are some submerged rocks. If you are going to double dip and have a swim from both beaches, just remember it is quite a long way across the sandy tombolo – over 150 metres at some points – so it can get quite chilly if it is windy.

If you'd like some company, it's certainly worth contacting the local swimming group – the Selkies – as some of their members live locally and swim here regularly.

TECHNICAL INFORMATION

DESCRIPTION **beach** ORIENTATION **north and south** TIDES **can swim at any time** ACCESS **sandy track to the beach** ENTRY **sand** GOOD FOR **normally having a sheltered side; longer swims up and down the bays; double dipping** LOCAL GROUP **Selkies** LOCATION **59.9706, -1.3346** AVOID **submerged rocks at the eastern end of the northern beach (59.9720, -1.3318)**

Getting there

From the A970 between Lerwick and Sumburgh, turn on to the B9122. Follow signs to *Bigton* and *St Ninian's Isle*, which will take you on to a narrow road. Once in Bigton, keep following signs towards *St Ninian's Isle* to reach the beach car park. While there are no facilities at the car park, there are public toilets in Bigton, opposite the community shop.

It is possible to link up the main Lerwick–Sumburgh bus with a bus to Bigton, stopping by the community shop. The buses aren't very regular, but it is great to be able to visit such an isolated place by public transport.

Refreshments

» **Bigton Community Shop**, Bigton. Friendly shop with plenty of local baked goods.
» **Hoswick Visitor Centre Cafe**, Hoswick. Great selection of hot drinks, home-made cakes and light meals. Also has a craft shop and lots of information about the surrounding area's history and heritage.

Skaw Beach, Unst

You can't go to Shetland without swimming at the most northerly beach in the UK, can you? Well, I certainly couldn't resist!

At 60.82 °N, Skaw Beach lies towards the northern tip of Unst, the northernmost inhabited island in the UK. In fact, it is even closer to the Arctic Circle than both Oslo and Bergen in Norway.

Getting off the Yell–Unst ferry, thick sea fog enveloped the whole island, reducing visibility to near zero. Rain lashed against the windscreen as we travelled further north along Unst's narrow, winding roads. As such, I wasn't expecting to see much when we got to the beach, but, by some miracle (or maybe just lucky timing),

1 Hester and a curious seal, Skaw Beach © Brian Stallwood   2 Eider ducklings   3 Skaw Beach © Brian Stallwood

the mist had lifted enough over the headland to reveal golden sand and rocky cliffs.

Seabirds swooped and squabbled as I made my way down to the water. Ducks bobbed up and down in the waves. Looking more closely, I realised it was an eider duck nursery – the females teaching a little flotilla of fluffy ducklings to ride the waves in the sheltered shallows before they were ready to head out into rougher seas.

While swimming, I watched the ducks moving away through the choppy water and spotted a couple of curious seals gazing at me from a distance, possibly wondering what this crazy human was doing bobbing about in the sea on a rainy, misty day in Shetland.

THE SWIM

This is probably more of a location for a quick dunk than a longer swim. When I arrived for my dip, there was a strong northerly breeze, and it was characteristically bouncy.

It's better to swim here around high tide when the beach entry is gently sloping. The angle of the beach changes further down, and the entry shelves off quite steeply towards low tide, meaning the waves may have a stronger undertow.

TECHNICAL INFORMATION

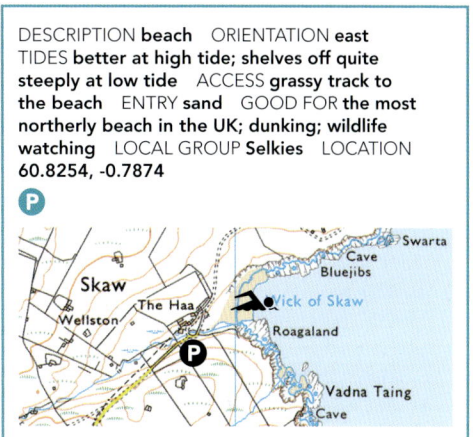

DESCRIPTION **beach**   ORIENTATION **east**
TIDES **better at high tide; shelves off quite steeply at low tide**   ACCESS **grassy track to the beach**   ENTRY **sand**   GOOD FOR **the most northerly beach in the UK; dunking; wildlife watching**   LOCAL GROUP **Selkies**   LOCATION **60.8254, -0.7874**

Getting there

To get to Unst from Mainland Shetland, you need to take two ferries, first crossing to Yell and then over to Unst. Once on Unst, head north on the A968, then turn on to the B9087 (signposted *Haroldswick*) until you see a small sign for *Skaw*. Follow this narrow road until you get to a small parking area.

Access

Access to the beach is over a small wooden bridge and along a grassy track. Please note, no dogs are allowed beyond the bridge due to the sensitive wildlife habitats.

Refreshments

» **Victoria's Vintage Tea Rooms**, Haroldswick. *The* place to go for post-swim treats on Unst. Great hot drinks and an amazing selection of cakes, including the most chocolatey chocolate cake I have ever had the pleasure of eating. Popular little place that can get surprisingly busy around lunchtime, but they also do takeaways.

» **Final Checkout Cafe**, A968, Balsasound. Handy little shop, cafe and fuel station with public toilets. Good for basic hot drinks and bacon rolls.

Brora Beach

Brora has two beaches, separated by the River Brora and its little tidal harbour. The south beach is wilder and rockier. It is accessed from the beach car park in Lower Brora and is quite exposed to the wind. This side can get big waves and is popular with surfers.

The north beach stretches for miles, with sand as far as you can see. It is definitely the better beach for swimming and the regular meeting place of the local swimming group. Accessed from the golf course, the beach is amazingly clean due to a community initiative to remove rubbish and is a Scotland's Beach Award beach.

Local swimmers have been lucky enough to spot porpoises feeding close to shore. Dolphins and minke whales have also been spotted further out at sea, and seals are regular visitors.

THE SWIM

Facing east, this is a fabulous spot for sunrise swims. When it is calm, the water is crystal clear and sparkling. The bay below the golf course is big enough for a decent swim – around 250 or 350 metres across, depending on the level of the tide. I prefer swimming at high tide, but you can swim any time. Make sure you steer clear of the mouth of the river where there can be submerged piles of rock.

If you are new to wild swimming, wondering about the conditions or looking for swim buddies, check out the local Brora Wild Swimming group, which can be found on Facebook. They often meet for sunrise swims and have a regular Saturday morning swim. They are a friendly and welcoming bunch and know the beach very well.

TECHNICAL INFORMATION

DESCRIPTION **beach**   ORIENTATION **east**
TIDES **can swim at any time**   ACCESS **short walk across the golf course to the beach**   ENTRY **sandy**
GOOD FOR **sunrise swims; wildlife spotting; short dips; longer swims**   LOCAL GROUP **Brora Wild Swimming**   LOCATION **58.0111, -3.8436**

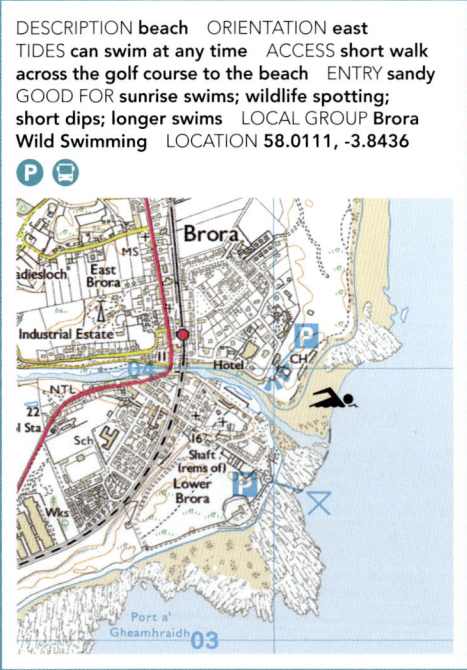

1 Miles of sand on Brora Beach © Shutterstock/Rob Atherton

Getting there

The A9 passes through the village of Brora, around 90 kilometres north-east of Inverness. In Brora, take the turning by the river, signposted to the *Golf Course* and *Beach*. This takes you down to a free public car park, shared with the golf club.

It is also possible to reach Brora by train and bus. It is a short walk from the railway station down to the beach.

Access

From the golf club car park, follow the little tracks through the golf course and down the dunes to the beach. Be mindful that there may be people playing golf – watch out when you cross the grass. Although the main beach stretches north for several kilometres, there is a smaller bay directly in front of the golf course which is excellent for swimming. Make sure you get in somewhere in the middle of the sandy bay as there may be submerged rocks at either side.

Refreshments

» **Cocoa Skye**, Brora. This little cafe and chocolate shop has brilliant hot chocolates and milkshakes, great waffles and artisan chocolates – pop in here for a real post-swim treat!
» **Linda's Cafe**, Brora. Small cafe with a simple menu – breakfasts, toasties and soup. Quick service, no-frills and relatively inexpensive. Good, hearty post-swim grub.

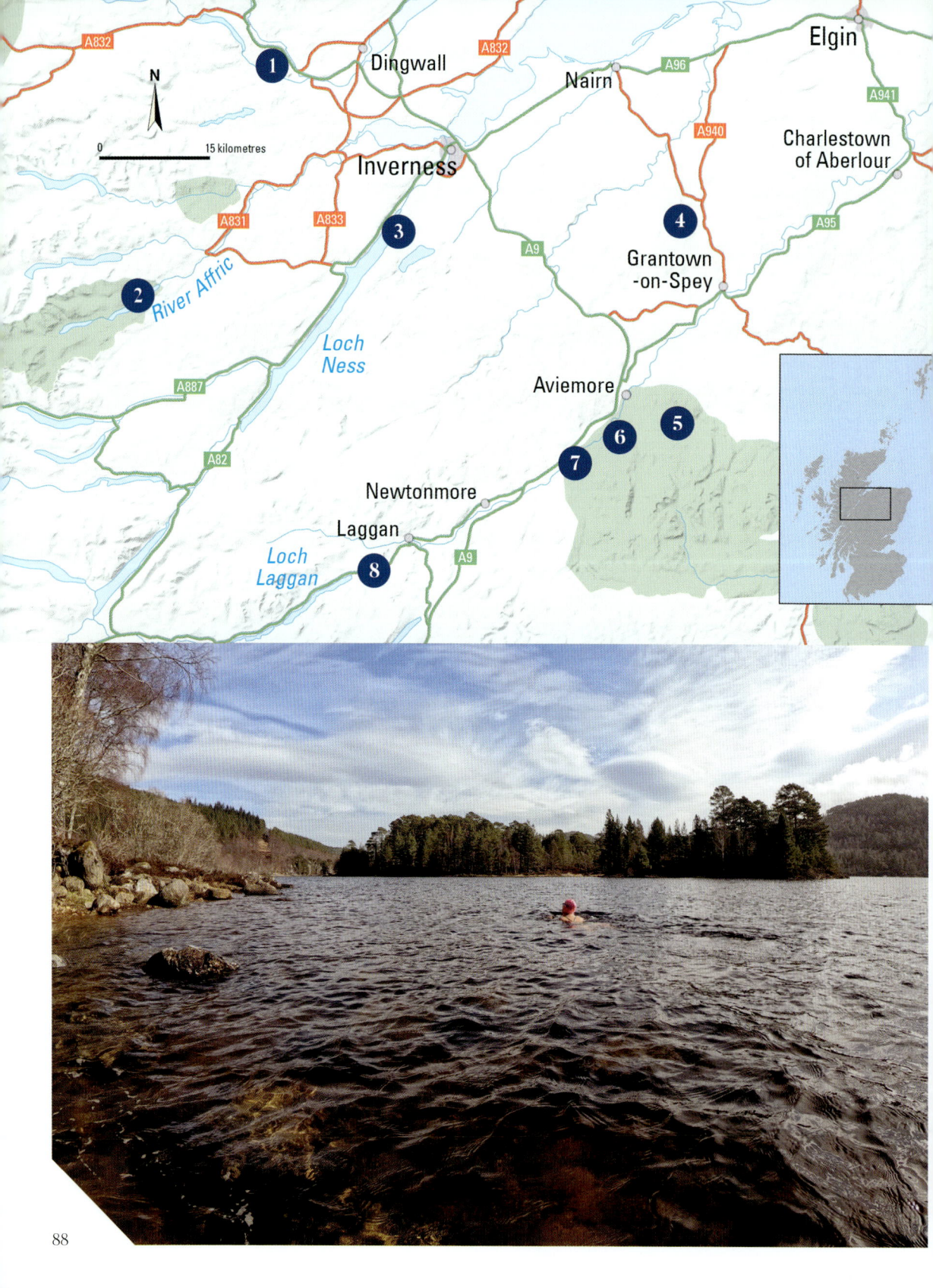

CENTRAL HIGHLANDS

Opposite Loch Beinn a' Mheadhoin

1 Loch Achilty   2 Moonlit Loch Achilty © Jeremy Hubbard   3 Loch Beinn a' Mheadhoin

Loch Achilty

Loch Achilty is a real Highland gem, loved by many local wild swimmers and visitors alike. It's a relatively small and shallow loch, set within sloping birch and oakwood forest, meaning it is generally pretty sheltered from the worst of the winds. I always find this loch friendly and welcoming and it is an excellent place for beginners to first dip their toes in the water: you can easily stay within your depth if you stick close to the car park end, and just swim up and down, close to shore. I've also used it as a location for long training swims when other places have been too wild, swimming loops of the loch with a support kayak.

THE SWIM

Loch Achilty is great for paddling and swimming in shallow water, but if you are happy to swim out of your depth, there is a little island with a couple of small trees towards the southern end of the loch, which makes a satisfying destination. A loop around the island is about 500 metres in total. If you want to do a longer swim, make sure you have a tow float and someone keeping an eye on you. It is amazing how sheltered it can be at the car park end while being a bit wild and wavy down at the other end.

TECHNICAL INFORMATION

DESCRIPTION **freshwater loch**   MAXIMUM DEPTH **36m**   LENGTH **1.4km**   MAXIMUM WIDTH **400m**   ELEVATION **40m**   ACCESS **short walk from the car park**   ENTRY **stony**   GOOD FOR **beginners; swimming around the island; post-swim picnics**   LOCAL GROUP **Achilty Swim and Cake Club; Inverness Open Water Swimming**   LOCATION **57.5698, -4.6306**

Getting there

Loch Achilty is near the village of Contin, north-west of Inverness on the A835. Follow signs to the loch from Contin; the forestry car park is on the left at the far end of the loch. There is no charge to park here but make sure you park in one of the designated places as it is a small car park and can get busy.

Access

Access to the loch is less than 50 metres from the car park. Follow the little path to the loch shore (it can be soggy underfoot after rain); the best place to get in is by the triangular picnic table. You can easily walk straight out into the loch from here, although it is pretty shallow and gravelly for a long time. Alternatively, you can get in the loch to the right of the table where it gets deeper more quickly.

Refreshments

There are some handy picnic benches for post-swim drinks and chats, so bring your own supplies. If you are more of a post-swim cafe kind of person, then there are a few good options close by.

» **Tarvies Cafe & Gift Shop**, A835. Not that inspiring from the outside, but this wee service station on the A835 always has a great selection of cakes, filled rolls and hot drinks.

» **Deli in the Square**, Strathpeffer. Friendly deli and cafe with delicious food and coffee.

» **Bad Girl Bakery**, Muir of Ord. If you are looking for the best cake in the area, it is worth dropping into this wee bakery in Muir of Ord for a treat! Also has delicious pies and sausage rolls.

Loch Beinn a' Mheadhoin

Glen Affric, where Loch Beinn a' Mheadhoin sits, is one of my favourite places in the world and worth a visit whether you plan to swim or not. Driving up the glen feels like stepping back in time. This is one of Britain's most extensive areas of ancient native woodland, the trees having first taken root about 10,000 years ago after the last ice age.

Loch Beinn a' Mheadhoin (pronounced Loch Ben-a-vey-an) means 'Loch of the Middle Hill'. It is a haven for wildlife and an exceptionally scenic, tranquil place to swim. The loch is also part of an ambitious hydroelectric scheme, which means water levels can change dramatically from one visit to the next. The nesting birds are provided with floating islands which ensure that they always have somewhere to shelter.

THE SWIM

The islands provide excellent protection from the wind whistling up the glen and make this a nice, sheltered spot for swimming. When the water level is high, it is roughly 75 metres over to the nearest island, straight across from the entry point.

To avoid disturbing nesting birds, don't get too close to the floating islands or scramble up on to the main islands between April and mid-September.

When the sun is shining through the water, it is worth dipping your face in and looking at the sparkling minerals (mica schist) glittering on the rocks.

TECHNICAL INFORMATION

DESCRIPTION **freshwater loch**   MAXIMUM DEPTH **50m**   LENGTH **8.5km**   MAXIMUM WIDTH **700m**   ELEVATION **220m**   ACCESS **short walk from the car park**   ENTRY **stony, gravelly or rocky (depends on water level)**   GOOD FOR **short dips; leisurely swims across to the islands; stunning scenery**   LOCATION **57.2923, -4.9149**

Getting there

Take the A831 to Cannich, then turn on to a minor road, signposted Glen Affric. Keep going for around 12 kilometres to reach Loch Beinn a' Mheadhoin car park on the left. There is no charge at this car park (unlike other Glen Affric car parks). There are also no facilities here, but there are toilets at Dog Falls (back towards Cannich) and the main Glen Affric car park (further up the glen).

Access

Follow the little path from the car park to the loch's edge. My preferred entry spot is directly opposite the tip of the nearest island, just in front of one of the picnic benches. The entry to the loch is rocky and can look quite different depending on the water level. You will need something protective on your feet.

Refreshment

It's best to use the picnic benches and bring your own supplies, but if you need to top up on cake or fancy a hot meal in a cafe, there are some options in nearby Tomich.

» **Sue's Cakes**, Tomich. A super little honesty cake shed in Tomich, just past the main village. Seasonal.
» **Coach House Cafe**, Tomich. Former village post office, now serving superb coffee, home-made cakes, snacks and light lunches. Seasonal.
» **The Tomich Hotel**, Tomich. The restaurant and cosy Black Pennell bar at the Tomich Hotel is where you need to go if you want some proper pub grub.

1 Loch Ness sign, Dores Beach **2** A breezy dip at Dores Beach

Dores Beach, Loch Ness

A bucket-list swim for many, Loch Ness was my introduction to the wild swimming community in Scotland. Before setting up my own local groups in the Cairngorms, I would join the Wild Highlanders for a dip at Dores Beach every Saturday morning. I made some wonderful friends and always marvelled at how hardy they all were swimming in such wild conditions all year round.

In 2015 I swam the length of the loch as part of a relay team. We swam the 36.3 kilometres overnight, and I remember being convinced that Nessie was going to eat me! Clearly, that didn't happen, and we made it to the other end only mildly hypothermic. I think I am still a little bit traumatised by the experience, but I still love swimming here, as long as no one makes me swim to the other end.

THE SWIM

You can get in anywhere along the beach, but I tend to get in at the concrete slipway just behind the Loch Ness sign. The entry is really stony, so make sure you wear something to protect your feet. It is quite a gently sloping entry to start with, but it does get deep reasonably quickly after the first ten metres or so.

Swimming in Loch Ness can be quite a daunting experience, especially if you are not used to swimming in dark water. You don't have to swim far from the shore to get into really deep water, which looks pitch black when you gaze down into the depths. If you are worried about the depth, you can swim parallel to the shore, still seeing the bottom, for a good 500-metre (one way) stretch along the beach.

Due to the massive volume of water in Loch Ness, the water temperature in summer is often colder than the surrounding lochs. Some years the loch barely reaches 10 °C in the middle of summer, although it can sometimes get up to 14 °C in warmer years.

1

2

TECHNICAL INFORMATION

DESCRIPTION **freshwater loch**   MAXIMUM DEPTH
227m   LENGTH **36km**   MAXIMUM WIDTH **2.7km**
ELEVATION **16m**   ACCESS **short walk to the beach**
ENTRY **stony**   GOOD FOR **playing in the waves;**
searching for Nessie!   LOCAL GROUP **Wild**
Highlanders; Inverness Open Water Swimming
SEPA BATHING WATERS **water quality tested**
June–September   LOCATION **57.3824, -4.3339**

Getting there

To get to Dores, head south from Inverness on
the B862. Buses run from Inverness to Dores,
but they aren't very frequent.

There is a car park right by the beach, but this
belongs to the Dores Inn and is for customers
only. However, if you plan to go there for a meal
or a drink after your swim (which I recommend),
you can park here. There is some roadside
parking near the inn or a free public car park a
short distance away next to the village church.

Refreshments

» **Dores Inn**, Dores. Cosy pub right next to
the loch. I have many fond memories of
post-swim hot chocolate huddles around
the wood-burning stove after my Loch Ness
Saturday morning swims.

» **The Spot**, Dores Beach. Cafe van permanently located at Dores Beach. Serves
excellent coffee and an assortment of
cakes.

Lochindorb

Lochindorb is another local favourite of mine,
with the added bonus of a ruined castle on
an island to swim out to. Nestled high up
on the bleak and beautiful Dava Moor, the
loch is somewhat exposed to the elements
meaning that swims here can be windswept and
interesting! In summer, the moor is a carpet of
purple heather, full of birds and other wildlife.
If you catch it on a rare still day, this is a popular
spot for paddleboarding and fishing.

The name Lochindorb comes from the Gaelic
Loch nan Doirb, meaning 'Loch of the Minnows'
or 'Loch of Trouble'. The castle is reputed to
date back to the 13th century and certainly saw
its fair share of action over the years. It was
occupied by English forces during the Wars of
Scottish Independence and, towards the end
of the 14th century, the castle was known as
'Wolf's Lair', as it was the stronghold of Alexander
Stewart, the infamous and terrifying Wolf of
Badenoch. In the 15th century, it was ordered, by
royal mandate, to be destroyed, although most
of the outer walls still stand at an impressive six
metres high and two metres thick today.

THE SWIM

The best entry point is opposite the castle. It is
stony with a gradual slope.

If you swim across to the island it's about 400
metres each way or one kilometre if you want
to swim around the island. The best view of the
castle ruins is from the northern shore, where
you can still see the remains of the impressive
round towers and the entrance to the walled
central quadrangular courtyard. If you are going
to get out and look around the island, make
sure you have something to protect your feet as
there are lots of sharp rocks and stinging nettles.

If it's windy, swimming back to your start
point can be tricky as the wind and waves often
push you further along the loch than you might

1 Lochindorb © Calum Maclean

anticipate. It is a good idea to leave something visible on the shore and aim to swim upwind to make sure you end up back in the right place.

TECHNICAL INFORMATION

DESCRIPTION **freshwater loch** MAXIMUM DEPTH **16m** LENGTH **3.3km** MAXIMUM WIDTH **900m** ELEVATION **295m** ACCESS **park beside the loch** ENTRY **stony** GOOD FOR **swimming to or around the castle** LOCATION **57.4038, -3.7048**

Getting there

You can access the loch from the single-track road that skirts the eastern side of the loch, connecting the A939 (Grantown-on-Spey to Nairn) with the B9007 (Carrbridge to Ferness). There are multiple lay-bys off the road adjacent to the loch, including several spaces for cars opposite the castle. These parking places can get busy with camper vans on sunny summer weekends, so you may need to park further along the loch. Please make sure you are not blocking any passing places or entrances.

Refreshments

» **KJ's Bothy Bakery**, Grantown-on-Spey. Don't be put off by the industrial estate location – you can get fantastic coffee and cake, yummy sandwiches and excellent sausage rolls here. If you are passing, stop here first and pick up something to scoff loch-side after your swim.

» **Logie Steading**, Dunphail. A great lunch or coffee stop on the road towards Forres. Beautiful gardens, cafe, farm shop and a collection of creative businesses.

» **The Croft Cafe**, Carrbridge. Great baking and hot drinks.

Loch Morlich

When it comes to wild swimming in Scotland, Loch Morlich was my first love. It is a perfect location for swimming, with its stunning sandy beach and reflections of the Cairngorms. In 2017, after struggling to find people in my local area to swim with, I set up the Cairngorm Wild Swimmers, and the rest is history! There is now a large group of hardy, year-round swimmers who meet on Saturday mornings for a swim and a blether. New swimmers and visitors are always welcome.

I have so many wonderful memories of swimming here – my first experiences of breaking the ice with a sledgehammer, training for long swims in the summer and taking new groups into the water for their first ever outdoor swims.

THE SWIM

The sandy beach has a gently sloping entry, shallow enough to stand (but deep enough to swim) until you get to around 15 metres from the shore when it shelves off and becomes deep very quickly. Ideally, get in the water to the left of the boats (summer only), so you don't get in the way of other water users.

It is possible to swim parallel to the shore for around 500 metres along the beach, meaning that you can easily do a kilometre (there and back) without ever going out into deeper water. In the summer, marker buoys make great circuits for longer swims. The water can get very busy with other water users on warm days in the summer, so it's best to go early or late to avoid the crowds.

1

TECHNICAL INFORMATION

DESCRIPTION **freshwater loch**   MAXIMUM DEPTH **15m**   LENGTH **1.6km**   MAXIMUM WIDTH **1km**
ELEVATION **320m**   ACCESS **short walk from the road/car park; sandy beach**   ENTRY **sand**   GOOD FOR
short dips; long swims; spectacular views of the mountains   LOCAL GROUP **Cairngorm Wild Swimmers**
SEPA BATHING WATERS **water quality tested June–September**   LOCATION **57.1673, -3.7026**

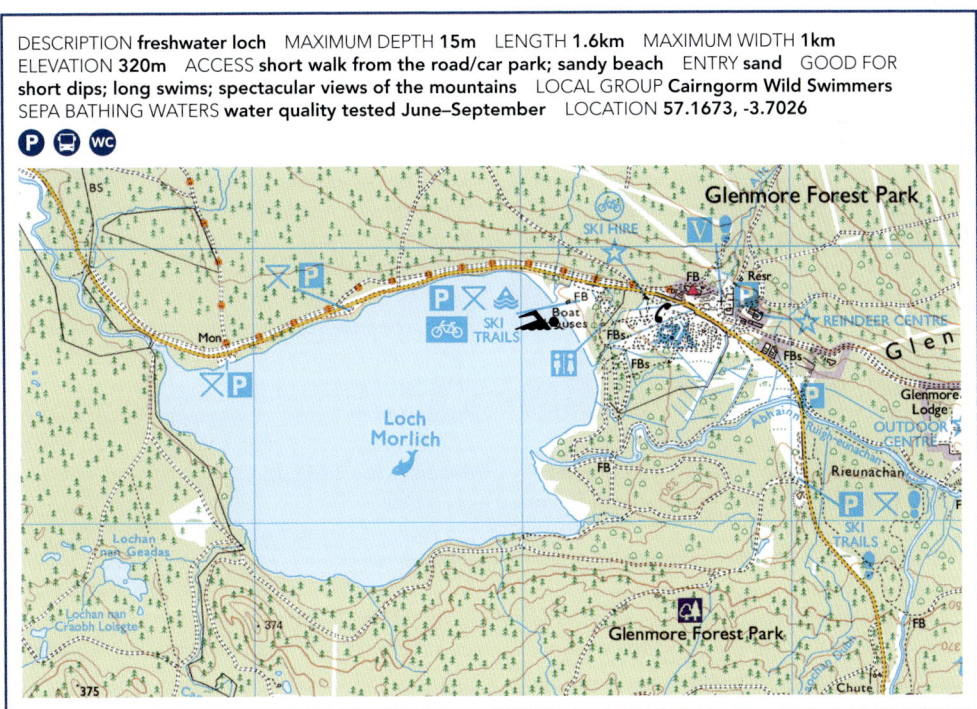

Getting there
Regular buses run between Aviemore and
Loch Morlich. If you are driving, take the B970
from Aviemore then turn off on to a minor
road at Coylumbridge, following signs towards
Glenmore. Follow the road for around seven
kilometres, passing the loch on the right-hand
side. The pay-and-display car park is at the far
end of the loch. You can also cycle from Aviemore
on the Old Logging Way. The loch, beach and car
parks can get extremely busy in the summer.

Notes
Loch Morlich Watersports have a webcam,
which is great for checking conditions before
you travel: *www.lochmorlich.com/webcam*
   While the loch can get really cold in the
winter, the fact it is relatively shallow means
that it can occasionally get blue–green algae in
late summer, coinciding with the warmest water
temperatures.

Refreshments
» **Boathouse Cafe**, Loch Morlich. Seasonal
   cafe, right on the beach above the
   watersports centre.
» **Cobbs Cafe**, Glenmore Visitor Centre.
   Large cafe with lots of seating inside and
   some picnic tables outside. Great hot
   chocolate and superior breakfast rolls.
» **Pine Marten Bar & Scran**, Glenmore.
   Lovely wee cafe and bar, with extra
   covered outside seating. Friendly staff,
   who occasionally dress as squirrels.

1 Handy branches to hang your kit from at Loch an Eilein   **2** Loch an Eilein © Nina Caudrey

Loch an Eilein

With its fairy-tale castle, spectacular mountain scenery and ancient Caledonian pine forest, Loch an Eilein really is the quintessential Highland swimming location. This used to be my lunchtime swim spot when I worked in an office down the road. Not many people can say they just popped out for a swim around a castle in their lunch break!

Loch an Eilein (pronounced Loch an Yellen) is Gaelic for 'Loch of the Island'. The castle on the island was probably built in the fourteenth century and added to in later centuries. It was used as a place of safety, where locals could hide from raiding clansmen who used the Thieves' Road to sneak down into Strathspey to steal cattle.

THE SWIM

The best entry point is a short walk from the car park, opposite the castle. You can get in at the northern end of the loch (next to the car park),
but you end up wading in very shallow water for about 50 metres.

From the car park, walk along the path towards the loch and when you get to the water, turn right and head along the main track for a few hundred metres until you see the castle on your left. The entry is somewhat rocky, with large stones underfoot. Protective footwear is essential. Once you have negotiated the stones, it shelves off fairly rapidly around ten metres from the shore.

It is around 60 metres out to the castle. While this may seem doable for even novice swimmers, the channel across to the castle is very black and peaty which can seem unnerving if you are not used to swimming in dark water. The distance is around 300 metres if you swim a loop of the castle island and back to where you started.

However tempting it is, please do not climb through the doorway and look around the castle island. The landowners are keen to prevent further deterioration of the castle ruins and keep the island as a sanctuary for nesting birds.

3 Winter dip, Loch an Eilein © Becca Harvey **4** Post-swim moment, Loch an Eilein © Becca Harvey

TECHNICAL INFORMATION

DESCRIPTION **freshwater loch** MAXIMUM
DEPTH **20m** LENGTH **1.6km** MAXIMUM WIDTH
500m ELEVATION **260m** ACCESS **500-metre
walk on a good track** ENTRY **rocky** GOOD
FOR **short dips; swimming around the castle;
spectacular views; wildlife watching** LOCAL
GROUP **Cairngorm Wild Swimmers** LOCATION
57.1494, -3.8232

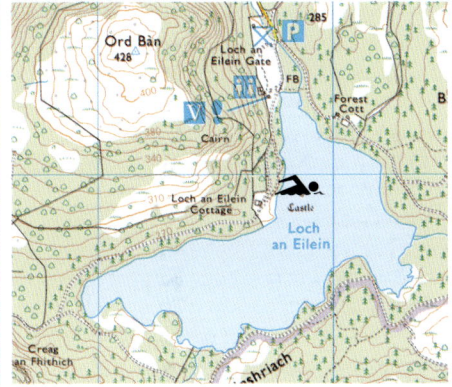

Getting there

The loch is well signed from the B970 between
Inverdruie and Feshiebridge. There is a charge
to park in the car park; the car park attendant
tends to be there from around 9 a.m. until
5 p.m. Alternatively, you could cycle from
Aviemore (six kilometres each way).

Refreshments

I usually take a hot drink with me for after my
swim, but there are some great local options
available courtesy of the Rothiemurchus estate.

» **Loch an Eilein Gallery**, Loch an Eilein.
   This little gallery showcases art from local
   craftspeople and also sells coffee, cold
   drinks and ice cream. Seasonal.
» **The Barn at Rothiemurchus**,
   Rothiemurchus Centre. Large cafe next to
   the Rothiemurchus Farm Shop. Lots of local
   produce and a good selection of cakes and
   hot drinks.

1 The author in an ice hole in Loch Insh **2** Clearing the ice, Loch Insh **3** An autumn dip, Loch Insh © Bernie McGee

Loch Insh

My local loch and my sanctuary (it was particularly important to me when restrictions due to the Covid-19 pandemic meant we were only allowed to travel a short distance from home); Loch Insh has a special place in my heart. There is a friendly watersports centre and restaurant overlooking the water, with stunning views, particularly at sunset. Even when the weather is terrible, it is a great place to swim due to the various undercover areas and a cosy cafe upstairs.

In winter, it is possible to shelter under the main balcony of the cafe. My local swimming group, the Loch Insh Dippers, also have their own Dippers Den – a small, covered outdoor changing area at the far end of the beach, tucked away at the end of the decking. It has hooks, benches and boards used to record water temperatures and leave messages. If it is vacant, please feel free to use it and leave us a message!

THE SWIM

You can get in anywhere along the beach, directly outside the watersports centre, when it is quiet. The entry is pebbly but does get more sandy as you head further out. It gets deeper gradually, and there are no sudden drop-offs.

The loch is very welcoming to swimmers, and out of hours, you can swim loops of the moored boats, around the buoys or along the shore in any direction. During busier times (watersports activities usually run from 10 a.m. until 5 p.m.), make sure you keep out of the way of other loch users. There is likely to be sailing, windsurfing and hydrofoiling going on in windier conditions, so it is best to keep to the left of the pontoons to avoid them. Swimming with a tow float is essential.

If you plan a longer swim in the summer, keep away from Tom Dubh island, as there are nesting ospreys that shouldn't be disturbed.

The Loch Insh Dippers swim every Sunday morning at the loch, with hot drinks and breakfast in the Boathouse afterwards. Visitors are very welcome!

TECHNICAL INFORMATION

DESCRIPTION **freshwater loch** MAXIMUM DEPTH **31m** LENGTH **1.7km** MAXIMUM WIDTH **950m**
ELEVATION **220m** ACCESS **from watersports centre** ENTRY **sandy/stony beach** GOOD FOR **swims around the boats; undercover changing area; post-swim food and drink; sunset swims** LOCAL GROUP **Loch Insh Dippers; Cairngorm Wild Swimmers** LOCATION **57.1167, -3.9213** AVOID **Tom Dubh island (57.1219, -3.9284)**

Getting there

Loch Insh is best accessed by car or bike. Take the B9152 to Kincraig and then follow the brown signs to *Loch Insh Watersports*. Parking for the watersports centre is well signed, with additional overflow parking in the summer. The centre is great and they're really supportive of swimmers – pop in and grab a drink or something to eat when you are there.

Refreshments

» **Boathouse Restaurant**, Loch Insh Outdoor Centre. This cosy cabin restaurant and bar overlooking the loch has a great selection of food and drink. I practically live there, so if you see someone sitting by the radiator in a blue robe and woolly hat, it is probably me!

» **Old Post Office Cafe**, Kincraig. A not very well-kept local secret, this little cafe is so good I almost don't want to tell you about it! Run by the Vastano family, the food is delicious, with daily specials and outstanding cakes.

Lower Pattack Falls

With the dark pool, rocky gorge and trees towering above, these waterfalls on the River Pattack have an otherworldly, prehistoric feel. It's easy to get carried away and think you are in the middle of nowhere, but this swimming spot is actually very accessible, close to the A86 near Kinloch Laggan.

If you take the upper path from the car park you get to a viewpoint, overlooking the river and gorge. I would always suggest going up here first to assess the river's flow before deciding whether to swim here. While the pool below the falls can be a tranquil swimming spot, I've also seen it raging like a dark, churning cauldron. If there are lots of bubbles and you don't think you would be able to swim right up to the falls, think again!

THE SWIM

To get to the access point from the car park, take the lower path to the right, which takes you down to the river. Providing the water level is low (which it needs to be if you are going to swim), there is a nice little sandy area for changing. Entry to the large pool is via a short section of the river, which is very stony underfoot (protective footwear recommended). Swim or wade upstream into the pool and then, after your swim, float back to where you started.

Once you are in the main pool, it is more of a float-around-and-play than a proper swim. Beneath the viewpoint, there is a cave in the rocks. This is a tunnel diverting water from the River Mashie via an aqueduct to join the River Pattack. Local kids have been known to dare each other to swim up the tunnel – this is definitely not recommended!

When the water levels are very low it is possible to swim right up to the waterfall and sit on the rocks to get a good waterfall shoulder massage. You can also scramble up the right-hand side of the waterfall to swim in the upper pool. Be careful as this can be extremely slippery; I normally end up sliding back down on my bottom.

2 Swimming into the dark pool © Becca Harvey

TECHNICAL INFORMATION

DESCRIPTION **river pool** RIVER **Pattack**
ELEVATION **260m** ACCESS **short walk from
the car park** ENTRY **sandy and then rocky**
GOOD FOR **pottering in the pool; playing; picnics;
floating on your back and soaking up the view**
LOCATION **56.9816, -4.3609**

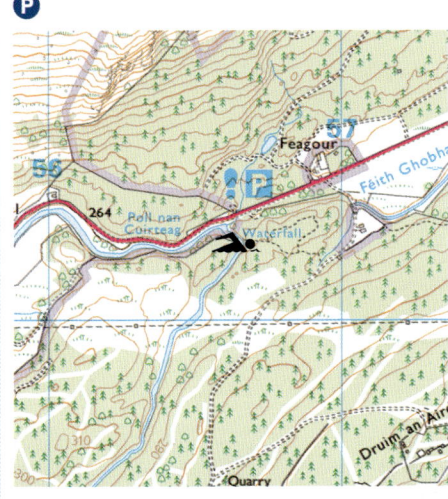

Getting there

The Lower Pattack Falls are easily accessible
by car, just off the A86 between Kinloch Laggan
and Strath Mashie. Keep a close eye out for
the car park as it can be easy to miss.

Refreshments

» **Laggan Wolftrax Cafe**, Laggan Forest
Trust, Laggan. Community-run cafe with
fabulous hot chocolate and some good
vegan options too. Seasonal.
» **Laggan Coffee Bothy**, Laggan. Former
village stores, now a cosy cafe (with a
wood-burning stove) in Laggan village.
» **Caoldair Coffee and Craft Shop**,
Laggan. Lovely cafe on the A889 towards
Dalwhinnie with indoor and outdoor
seating and great views. Fabulous cakes,
coffees, toasties, soup and cheese scones.

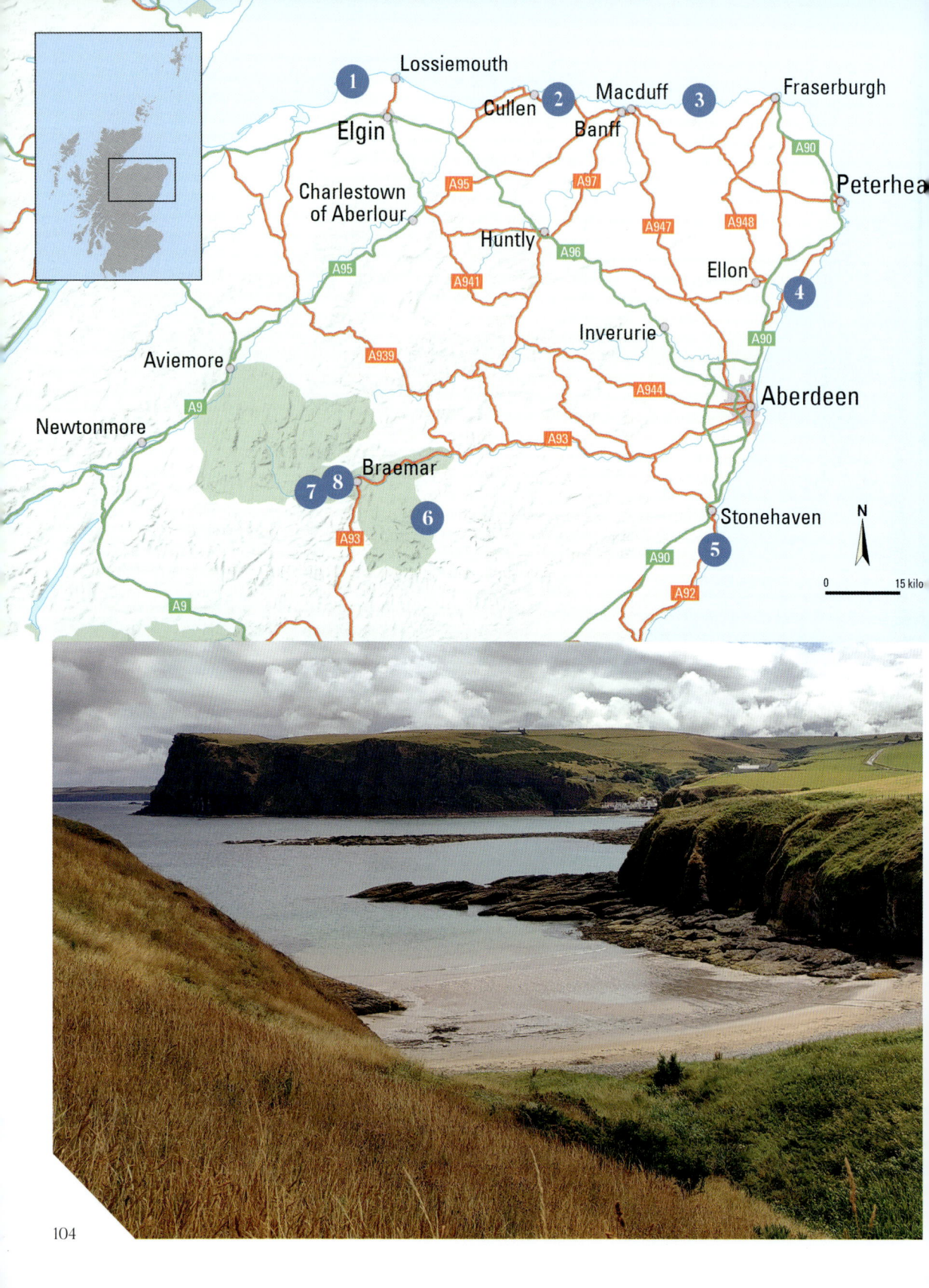

THE EAST

Opposite Cullykhan Bay

Hopeman & Clashach Cove

The Moray Coast is my closest place to access the sea, and I am lucky that it has many beautiful beaches to choose from. Although there are lots of alternatives, Hopeman is my favourite place to visit as it offers so many options for swimming. The high-walled Harbour juts out into the sea, protecting the beaches to the east and west (depending on the wind direction) and meaning that there is often a sheltered side to swim on. When the wind is blowing in from the north, the Harbour itself can be a calm place to dip. If you fancy a bit more of an adventure, Clashach Cove is only a 1.5-kilometre walk along the rocky coastline and has fascinating caves and rock formations to explore.

I love swimming here. The water is always crystal clear and full of underwater delights – crabs scuttling along the bottom, baby squid and schools of tiny fish. If you are lucky, you might catch a glimpse of the playful bottlenose dolphins who regularly travel up and down this coast.

WEST BEACH

This is the most popular swimming beach for local swimmers. It's a lovely wide bay, backed by dunes, often with gently rolling waves and enough space to swim a few lengths parallel to the beach. The bay is around 200 metres across at high tide and just over 100 metres across at low tide. Watch out for submerged rocks around the edges, including ones jutting out from the Harbour wall.

HARBOUR

The eastern basin of the Harbour can be an oasis of calm on wild winter days when the other beaches are unswimmable. It is only suitable for swimming outside busy times, due to activity in and around the Harbour. The entry is sandy and gently sloping. It is best around high tide, when it is around 100 metres from the beach to the back wall.

EAST BEACH

There are two sandy areas to the east of the Harbour, separated by a rocky area in the centre.

Do not swim at Findlay's Bay, closest to the Harbour, as it is well known for strong currents converging around the Harbour. There used to be lots of signage to say this, but not all of this has been reinstated.

Instead, stick to the far eastern section of the bay, beyond the beach huts. There is a gorgeous sandy beach, and the water is stunningly clear. Watch out for submerged rocks at the far end of the bay and the small tidal island (The Scailies), which is surrounded by kelp in the centre. Keep within the bay and do not swim past or around the headland to the east.

CLASHACH COVE

To reach Clashach Cove, start at the road behind East Beach and follow the path to the east, signed *Coastal Path*. Ignore a turning on the right towards the Braemou Well and follow the path, which takes you along the coast and skirts around the edge of the golf course before climbing up some steps. Once you have climbed the hill, fork left to descend to Clashach Cove. The track is steep in places and mainly sandy.

This cove below Clashach Quarry is a most idyllic spot. When the sun is shining, you might think you've landed in the Mediterranean. The sandy bay is topped by pebbles and surrounded by sandstone cliffs dotted with caves, tunnels and even a small natural arch. At low tide, the entry is sandy and gently sloping.

TECHNICAL INFORMATION

DESCRIPTION **beach** ORIENTATION **north and north-west** TIDES **best around slack tide; Harbour best at high tide** ACCESS **short walk to beaches in Hopeman or longer walk (1.5 kilometres) to Clashach Cove** ENTRY **sand** GOOD FOR **multiple options; sheltered swims; dolphin spotting** LOCAL GROUP **Houpmin Trouts; Moray Wild Swimmers** LOCATION **West Beach 57.7097, -3.4392; Harbour 57.7111, -3.4361; East Beach 57.7115, -3.4272; Clashach Cove 57.7134, -3.4126** AVOID **Findlay's Bay (directly east of the Harbour)**

Getting there

Hopeman is on the B9040 between Burghead and Lossiemouth. From the B9040, turn into the village following signs to the *Beach* and the *Harbour* along Harbour Street. At the bottom of the hill, either turn left to park by the Harbour (if it is quiet) or turn right towards two further small car parks.

Regular buses run between Elgin and Burghead stopping at Hopeman. The bus stop is up on the B9040, around 500 metres from the Harbour.

Refreshments

» **The Boatyard**, Hopeman. Lovely little food cabin by East Beach. Excellent hot chocolate and exceptional cakes. Very swimmer friendly and, as a bonus, it is run by a swimmer too!
» **Hopeman Sands Coffee Shop**, Hopeman. Great cafe for a post-swim hot drink and cake or lunch.
» **Stew 'n' Drew's**, Hopeman. Excellent ice cream shop with a great variety of flavours.

Sandend Beach

Nestled on Scotland's north-east coast, the small 17th-century fishing village of Sandend is a magnet for surfers who travel far and wide to ride the waves crashing on to its long sandy beach. While surfing beaches are generally not great swimming beaches, on calm days, when the wind is blowing from the south or south-west, this can be a magical place to dip and enjoy the sea.

THE SWIM

It's only a short walk down to the beach from the road, but it can be another 200 metres out to the water at low tide.

While this is mainly a surfing beach, it can be sheltered and lovely for swimming. The entry is sandy (with occasional stones) and gently sloping. Enjoy playing in the waves and lovely swims parallel to the beach. Make sure you stay away from the rocky edges of the bay

1 Sandend Beach © Shutterstock/Dale Lorna Jacobsen

– especially the west side (near the village) as there can be currents flowing back out to sea along this edge.

There is a surf school located on the beach, so watch out for beginner surfers and paddleboarders. The beach is huge and there is plenty of space for everyone.

TECHNICAL INFORMATION

DESCRIPTION **beach**   ORIENTATION **north**
TIDES **possible to swim at any time**   ACCESS **short walk to the beach**   ENTRY **sand**   GOOD FOR **playing in the waves; swims in the bay** LOCAL GROUP **Banffshire Coast Swimmers; Wild Dookers**   LOCATION **57.6837, -2.7441** AVOID **rocky edges; N, NE or NW winds**

Getting there

Sandend is a short distance off the A98 between Cullen and Portsoy and a 16-kilometre cycle (mainly along Sustrans National Route 1) along the coast from Buckie.

If you are driving, the village is signposted from the A98. There is a small gravelly public car park next to the holiday park. There are public toilets next to the car park.

Sandend can be reached by bus from nearby towns. The bus stop is a short walk from the beach.

Notes

If the main beach is too rough, it is sometimes possible to swim in the easy basin of the harbour which is more protected. Watch out for boat traffic and only attempt this at quiet times. The entry is stony so make sure you have something to protect your feet.

Refreshments

» **Lily's Kitchen Cafe**, Cullen. Surely the obvious thing to do after your swim is to go for a warming bowl of Cullen skink in Cullen! Lily's Kitchen is famous for this smoked haddock soup; other food is also available.

» **Symposium Coffee House**, Portsoy. Great place for coffee and pancakes and excellent hot chocolate.

Cullykhan Bay

People had told me about the beautiful beach of Cullykhan Bay for a while. The first time I arrived in the car park, it was pouring with rain, I couldn't see the beach, and I didn't know what all the fuss was about. As soon as I started walking down the path and got my first sight of the sea below, I fell in love with Cullykhan Bay.

Tucked into an inlet and sheltered by a rocky promontory to the north, it is a perfect combination of sandy beach, calm water, rocks and caves – perfect for paddling in the shallows, enjoying a longer swim or exploring the nooks and crannies around the edge. The headland above the beach also has a fascinating history and was once home to an Iron Age fort and a medieval castle. I'm already looking forward to my next visit!

THE SWIM

I like swimming here at high tide, but it is possible to dip here at any time. On my most recent visit, it was a very low tide, and I had a lovely dip, potter and float around, which was fabulous – I just didn't swim very far.

At high water, it's around 200 metres out from the beach to the mouth of the bay, so there is a large, sheltered area to swim in. If it is wavy, stick to the centre of the bay as there are rocks around the edges. If it is very calm, it is nice to potter around the edges and look into all the submerged rock pools and caves.

I would strongly advise staying within the bay. The currents can be quite strong between Troup Head and Pennan. If you decide to go out further than the bay, only do so in flat calm conditions, on a slack tide and take a tow float.

The walk back up to the car should help to warm you up again!

TECHNICAL INFORMATION

DESCRIPTION **beach**   ORIENTATION **east**
TIDES **possible to swim at any time**   ACCESS **250m downhill walk to the beach; good path, steep in places**   ENTRY **sand**   GOOD FOR **sheltered dips; exploring the rocks and caves**   LOCAL GROUP **Aberdeenshire Open Water Swimming**   LOCATION **57.6845, -2.2738**   AVOID **N or NE winds**

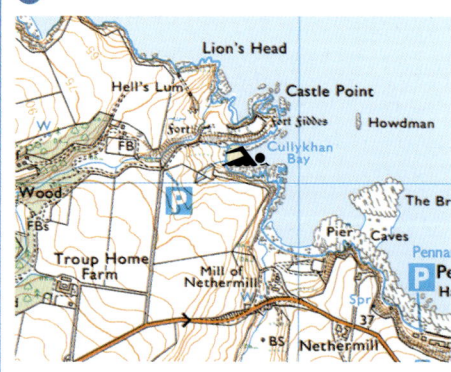

Getting there
Cullykhan Bay is signed off the B9031 around one kilometre west of the village of Pennan on the North Aberdeenshire coast. There is a large car park; there are no facilities.

Access
There is a good, well-worn track down to the beach from the car park. This includes a long boardwalk section with some steps. Be careful as it can be slippery after rain.

Refreshments
» **Coastal Cuppie**, Pennan. Wee shed by Pennan Harbour selling yummy traybakes, scones and hot drinks. Seasonal.
» **Eli's Coffee, Cakes and Crafts**, Gardenstown. Cosy little cafe with tasty soup and cakes.

1 Cullykhan Bay © Jane Sendall **2** Post-swim ice cream at Collieston Bay
3 Cullykhan Bay © Jane Sendall **4** Collieston Bay © Shutterstock/Kristin Greenwood

Collieston Bay

With its sandy beach and protective pier, Collieston Bay is a little sea swimmers' safe haven, surrounded by rough cliffs and unpredictable seas. Collieston was originally established as a fishing village in the 15th century but the fishing industries declined as the harbour filled up with silt over the years. What remains is a peaceful village with a wonderfully sheltered beach now popular with families, swimmers and paddleboarders. It is a gorgeous place to swim and a popular spot for locals and visitors alike.

THE SWIM

Access to the beach is via a concrete slipway, and the entry is gently sloping and sandy. Although occasionally breached during fierce winter storms, the long pier protects the bay from much of the weather coming in from the north and east, and a rocky headland protects the bay from the south-west.

At high tide, the sheltered swimming area is at its largest, and it's best to swim close to the walls on the bay's eastern side. There are some rocks towards the centre and the western side which become submerged at high water; you'll want to avoid these. At high tide, it's around 100 metres from the entry at the base of the slipway to the end of the long part of the pier wall. I've also dipped here at low tide, and it was still lovely, just a smaller area to swim. Do not venture out of the protected area, and watch out for boats near the pier.

I've always found the water to be quite cloudy when I've swum here. Not dirty, just full of silt and sediment. Thankfully this is a SEPA Bathing Waters testing site, so it is easy to check the water quality before you swim.

TECHNICAL INFORMATION

DESCRIPTION **beach/harbour** ORIENTATION **south-east** TIDES **best around high tide, but possible any time** ACCESS **concrete ramp down to beach** ENTRY **sand; gently sloping** GOOD FOR **sheltered dips; short swims** LOCAL GROUP **Aberdeenshire Open Water Swimming; Swim Free Aberdeen** SEPA BATHING WATERS **water quality tested June–September** LOCATION **57.3477, -1.9339**

Getting there

Collieston is to the north of Aberdeen, between Newburgh and Bay of Cruden. The village is well signed off the A975. Once in the village, follow signs for the *Harbour* and park at the pier. Parking here is convenient but limited. There is an additional, larger car park on a headland to the east of the village. From here, follow the signs for *Harbour & Village*, and it's around a 350-metre walk down to the beach.

Refreshments

» **Smugglers Cone**, Collieston. Not just ice cream! Also serves hot chocolates, paninis and snacks. Seasonal.
» **The Coffee Apothecary**, Ellon. A bit further away but exceptional coffee and a mouth-watering selection of cakes. Amazing hot chocolate.

Catterline Bay

Swooping seabirds and curious seals are my favourite memories from bobbing around in the sea at Catterline Bay. Sheltered from all but strong easterly or southeasterly winds, this curved bay is a fabulous spot to swim. Catterline is a historic fishing village, but it also has a history of smuggling, as the fishermen looked for ways to supplement their meagre income. Now the bay seems pretty quiet, apart from the odd small creel boat and a scattering of divers, swimmers and paddleboarders at weekends.

THE SWIM

The entry is relatively stony and slopes off quite sharply. Make sure you have something protective on your feet – ideally something with a bit of grip, as the stones can be pretty slippery. It's best to swim around high tide. The bay is approximately 250 metres across; keep within the bay and do not swim past the rocky outcrop to the south. Watch out for submerged rocks towards the far end of the beach.

Keep an eye out for boats and wear a tow float. I've never experienced any marine traffic while swimming here, other than a few paddleboarders and some nosy seals, but there are a few small boats moored up, and this is where the local diving club regularly meets in the summer.

1 Catterline Bay

TECHNICAL INFORMATION

DESCRIPTION **beach/harbour** ORIENTATION **east** TIDES **best around high tide** ACCESS **close to harbour-side parking** ENTRY **rocky; can be slippery** GOOD FOR **sheltered swims; sunrise dips; seal spotting** LOCAL GROUP **Aberdeenshire Open Water Swimming; Swim Free Aberdeen** LOCATION **56.8954, -2.2153**

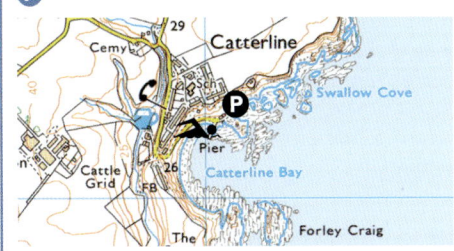

Getting there

Catterline is around eight kilometres south of Stonehaven and signed off the A92. Continue along the no-through road into the village and take the lower road, curving left, down towards the bay.

The road down to the harbour is very narrow and steep. There is a small amount of parking at the top of the slope if you don't fancy driving down. Parking at the bottom is limited, with a couple of spaces by the beach and room for four or five cars past the white boathouse.

Please note that the local dive club owns the boathouse and bothy and has regular dive meets here throughout the summer on Wednesday evenings and Sundays. There are likely to be more cars down in the small car park at these times. Check before driving down the hill!

Refreshments

» **Creel Inn**, Catterline. The only option in Catterline. A bit fancier than your standard local pub, with great seafood and a good selection of beers. Great views across the bay.

Alternatively, there are lots of options in Stonehaven, which is only a short drive away to the north. While you are there, why not check out Stonehaven's fabulous heated open-air swimming pool for an extra outdoor dip! It is open from early June until early September and they've even started doing late-night swim sessions (open until midnight) on some summer evenings.

» **The Villa Coffee Shop**, Stonehaven. Friendly cafe with excellent baking and yummy meals.
» **The Bay Fish & Chips**, Stonehaven. Rustic cabin for traditional fish and chips on the beachfront promenade.

1 A chilly dip in Loch Muick **2** Loch Muick © Shutterstock/iweta0077 **3** The view from the Loch Muick boathouse

Loch Muick

Loch Muick (pronounced 'Loch Mick') has royal connections and is part of the Balmoral Estate. Queen Victoria used to enjoy fishing trips on the loch and built a lodge along the western shore, where she spent a lot of time after the death of Prince Albert.

I love swimming here. It is stunning, and usually rather wild and bleak whenever I have visited. It is a good two-kilometre walk (on good tracks) from the car park to the loch, and there are many more paths if you fancy circumnavigating the loch or heading up into the surrounding hills.

THE SWIM

You can get in anywhere along the northern shore; however, it is quite a stony entry, and there is no shelter. My preferred entry place is a little further along the track (around 500 metres beyond the bridge), where there is a boathouse and a pebbly and sandy beach. The entry is pretty shallow to start with but eventually gets deep enough to swim.

You can swim anywhere you like in the loch – it can be pretty choppy when there is a south-westerly wind.

TECHNICAL INFORMATION

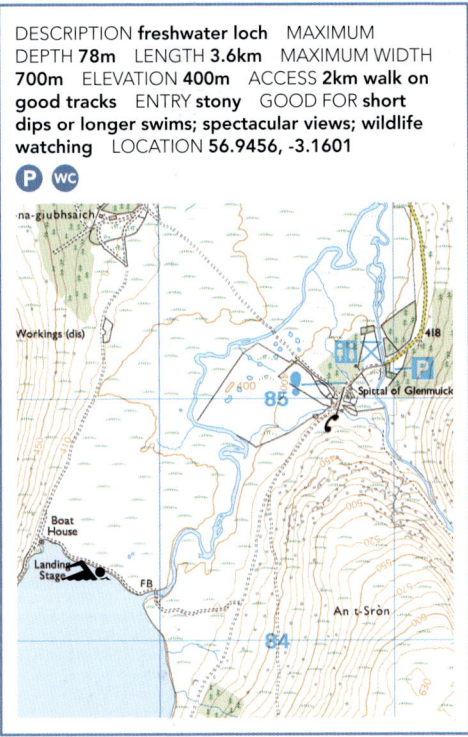

DESCRIPTION **freshwater loch**   MAXIMUM
DEPTH **78m**   LENGTH **3.6km**   MAXIMUM WIDTH
700m   ELEVATION **400m**   ACCESS **2km walk on
good tracks**   ENTRY **stony**   GOOD FOR **short
dips or longer swims; spectacular views; wildlife
watching**   LOCATION **56.9456, -3.1601**

Getting there

From Ballater, head across the bridge over the
River Dee, turn right and follow the B976 for a
short distance before turning left, following the
signpost for *Glen Muick*. Follow this road for
around 11 kilometres all the way to its end and
the car park (there is a parking charge) at the
Spittal of Glenmuick. There are toilets in the
car park during the summer months.

During extremely busy periods, when the
car park is full, the rangers may close the road
at the junction with the B976. Up-to-date information regarding road closures is posted on the
Balmoral Castle social media platforms.

Access

From the car park, walk over the bridge and
past the visitor centre building; keep heading in
the same direction (south) until you can see the
loch and the path splits. Take the right-hand,
lower, path and then turn right again. This path
takes you over a bridge and to the northern
shore of the loch.

Refreshments

Due to the longer walk to Loch Muick, make
sure you take your own post-swim hot drinks
and snacks. Head to Ballater if you want something more substantial to eat after your swim.

» **Brown Sugar Cafe**, Ballater. My go-to
quick stop for a hot drink and a cake.
Simple, light lunches, home-made soup
and home baking.

» **Bridge House Cafe**, Ballater. Fabulous
dog-friendly cafe. Perfect for brunch or
lunch. Indulgent hot chocolate, jumbo
sausage rolls and delicious sweet and
savoury pancakes.

There are plenty of other excellent establishments in Ballater, including **Bean for Coffee?
and The Bothy**.

Linn of Dee

A spectacular swimming spot on the River Dee with a deep gorge and beautiful water. The entire length of the River Dee is designated as a Special Area of Conservation due to its importance for wildlife, including salmon, otters and freshwater pearl mussels. The best swimming spot is downstream of the impressive Gothic-style bridge. This is the highest crossing point on the River Dee and was opened by Queen Victoria in 1857.

I have been to this area many times as a starting point for walks across the Cairngorms, but I've only been able to swim here on a handful of occasions. When river levels are running high, the gorge can be incredibly treacherous and unsuitable for swimming. Sadly, people have lost their lives in the fast-flowing water.

If you catch it in the right conditions, this is the most incredible swimming location. The underwater visibility here is exceptional, so make sure you take goggles to fully appreciate the experience. The water can be crystal clear with a hint of green or turquoise, or sometimes a bit darker with a hint of peat. The underwater rock patterns are pretty spectacular, and the mica schist embedded in the rock sparkles on sunny days. The deepest sections of the gorge (at around nine metres) are like swimming over a bottomless abyss. Keep your eyes peeled and you might see trout or salmon swimming upstream.

THE SWIM

The easiest entry and exit point is around 120 metres downstream of the bridge, where the river widens and there is a sandy and stony beach area. You can follow the boardwalk to get down to the beach. Here there are some lovely deeper pools to paddle and potter about in. It is also possible (although not always easy) to swim upstream, against the flow, into the gorge.

The other option is to find the shelving section of rock around 60 metres downstream of the bridge, and scramble down to a narrow, deep section of the river. Here you can get in and swoosh downstream to exit at the beach. Do not ever try and swim upstream from here – the narrowest section towards the bridge is known as the 'washing machine' and has dangerous circular currents and is not safe for swimming.

As with all rivers, only swim if water levels are very low. As a general rule, if it looks like anything other than a calm pool, then don't even think about swimming.

TECHNICAL INFORMATION

DESCRIPTION **river gorge/pool** RIVER **Dee** ELEVATION **360m** ACCESS **short walk on a good track** ENTRY **rocky** GOOD FOR **paddling; river swooshes; underwater exploring** SEPA WATER LEVEL **Dee (Grampian)@Mar Lodge: the levels really need to be 'low' to safely swim here** LOCATION **56.9885, -3.5440**

Getting there

To get to the Linn of Dee, head west from Braemar, following the River Dee for around ten kilometres before crossing a bridge and following signs to the car park.

There is a large National Trust for Scotland car park at the Linn of Dee. There is a parking charge if you're not a member; all proceeds go towards the conservation and maintenance of the estate. There are toilets in the car park during the summer months.

1 Swimming upstream at Linn of Dee © Alastair Goodridge   **2** Floating downstream at Linn of Dee © Alastair Goodridge
3 The gorge, Linn of Dee © Alastair Goodridge

Access

Cross the road opposite the entrance to the car park and follow the small track down to the river, signposted *Linn of Dee*.

Refreshments

The Linn of Dee is a reasonable drive away from the nearest cafes. Make sure you have your own supplies and a flask for after your swim. Braemar has several good places for refuelling on cake and hot chocolate, or for lunch.

» **The Bothy**, Braemar. My favourite cafe in Braemar, mainly because it connects to the excellent Braemar Mountain Sports and I love a bit of outdoor kit browsing! The cafe has a simple menu of tasty food and great views over the river if you sit on the patio out the back.

» **Gordon's Tearoom**, Braemar. One of the oldest establishments in the historic village of Braemar, this is an excellent place for post-swim hot drinks and has delicious home-made cakes and scones.

» **Hazelnut Pâtisserie**, Braemar. Run by the lovely Mathilde and Ros, this is the place to go for superior patisserie, perfect pies and excellent coffee. Seasonal.

Linn of Quoich

A little further along the quiet back road from the Linn of Dee is another stunning river pool, close to where Quoich Water joins the River Dee.

There is a curious, water-sculpted round carved hole known as the Punch Bowl in the rocks above the pool. This was reputedly used by the Earl of Mar as a punch bowl to celebrate successful deer hunts or for toasting the Jacobites.

When river levels are low, the river pool below the Punch Bowl is astonishingly turquoise and tempting!

THE SWIM

This is quite a small, shallow pool, so it is more of a place to play than to swim any distance. However, it can be fun to swim up against the waterfall current in your own natural endless swimming pool. The water clarity is superb, so make sure you take goggles to admire the incredible underwater rock patterns and sparkling, bubbly water.

I have seen photos of people getting into the Punch Bowl and swimming out into the river (or vice versa) – this is not a good idea as you

1

could easily get trapped or pulled out into the turbulent flow.

Of course, as with the Linn of Dee (see pages 116–117), it isn't always possible to swim here. Only consider swimming here if the pool in front of the Punch Bowl looks calm and tranquil, and you can clearly see the rocks and pebbles on the bottom.

TECHNICAL INFORMATION

DESCRIPTION **river pool**   RIVER **Quoich Water**
ELEVATION **350m**   ACCESS **short walk on a
good track**   ENTRY **rocky**   GOOD FOR **paddling;
swimming against the flow; picnics**   LOCATION
57.0045, -3.4592

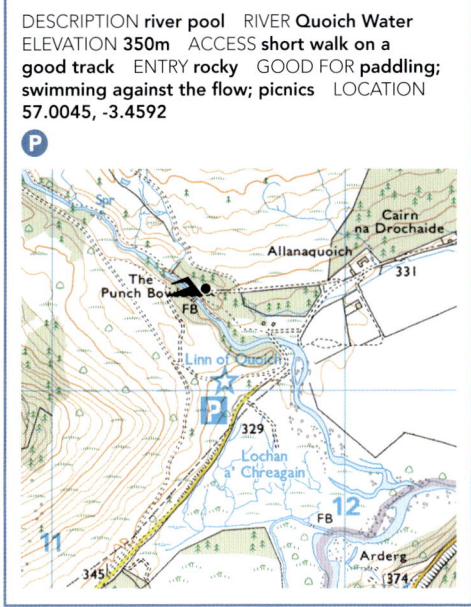

Getting there
The Linn of Quoich is around six kilometres further along the single-track road from the Linn of Dee. There is a small National Trust for Scotland car park; there is a parking charge if you're not a member.

Access
The quickest way to get to Linn of Quoich from the car park is to cross over Quoich Water via the bridge and follow the path close to the eastern bank of the river for about ten minutes until you reach an old stone cottage. The swimmable pool at the Linn of Quoich is just down the grassy slope below the cottage, in front of the narrow wooden footbridge.

You can access the pool from either side. I have always crossed the narrow footbridge and stepped down the rock ledges on the Punch Bowl (western) side of the river.

Notes
Although generally quieter than the nearby Linn of Dee, the grassy area between the cottage and the pool can be popular with wild campers during busy periods.

Refreshments
There aren't any cafes near the Linn of Quoich so bring your own supplies. If you fancy a coffee and cake afterwards, there are some ideas in nearby Braemar on page 117.

PERTHSHIRE, LOCH LOMOND & THE TROSSACHS

Opposite Loch Lomond © Shutterstock/richardjohnson

1 Pebbly entry at Soldier's Leap © Alastair Goodridge   **2** Swimming towards the Gorge © Susanne Masters

Soldier's Leap, Killiecrankie

Surrounded by ancient woodland and dramatic angular rocks, swimming in the River Garry at Soldier's Leap takes you back to the time of the Jacobites. The gorge is named after a soldier who, legend has it, successfully leapt across the gorge to freedom after the Battle of Killiecrankie in 1689. When the water levels are low, it is a peaceful place to explore, the peace only occasionally interrupted by a train rumbling over the viaduct. The only thing I've seen leaping here has been the occasional salmon!

THE SWIM

The entry is pebbly and gently sloping but gets reasonably deep by the time you enter the gorge.

You can either just dip in the calm pool at the gorge's entrance or swim upstream into the narrower channel, which is around 100 metres long. There are several pools and rocky sections to explore.

TECHNICAL INFORMATION

DESCRIPTION **river gorge/pool**   RIVER **Garry**
ELEVATION **100m**   ACCESS **500m walk with steep sections, uneven steps and a stream crossing**   ENTRY **pebbly**   GOOD FOR **upstream swims; beautiful views; exploring the gorge**
LOCAL GROUP **The Dell Dippers; Perthshire Wild Swimmers**   SEPA WATER LEVEL **Garry (Tayside)@ Killiecrankie: the levels really need to be 'low' to safely swim here**   LOCATION **56.7419, -3.7739**

Getting there

The village of Killiecrankie is seven kilometres north of Pitlochry. Pitlochry has good rail links; you can get the bus from Pitlochry to Killiecrankie and walk the short distance to the river. Killiecrankie is also accessible by bus from the nearby towns of Aberfeldy and Struan. If arriving by car, there is a large car park at the Killiecrankie Visitor Centre (pay and display); there are toilets in the visitor centre.

Access

From the car park, follow the track that heads down the hill and, when the path splits, take the left-hand turning. Follow signs to *Pass of Killiecrankie* and *River Tummel* (not *Soldier's Leap*, although it is worth the detour to see the viewpoint).

Once you're alongside the viaduct, cross the wooden bridge and, after a couple more arches, look for a little, unmarked track on the right, taking you down to the pebbles. Here you will have to cross a small stream (using rocks as stepping stones) before getting to the middle pebbly beach at the entrance to the gorge. If you can't cross the stream here, the water level is likely too high for swimming.

Refreshments

» **JacoBite Cafe**, Killiecrankie Visitor Centre. Handy cafe with surprisingly good cakes and patisserie. There are also information boards and a wee shop.

» Of course, there are also plenty of options in nearby Pitlochry. My favourites include **Hettie's Tearoom** and the **Salmon Leap Cafe** at the Pitlochry Dam Visitor Centre.

Loch Tay

Loch Tay is a magnificent stretch of dark water flanked by the impressive bulk of the Ben Lawers mountain range. It is a fascinating loch, steeped in history. Ancient settlers once lived on Loch Tay, inhabiting artificially created islands known as crannogs. There are around 18 crannogs on Loch Tay, one of which you can swim to from Dalerb.

The loch feels like my second home as I spend lots of time travelling backwards and forwards to the loch while organising and running the Scottish Winter Swimming Championships at Taymouth Marina. I've had many dips here in winter but also enjoyed longer summer swims. The loch can become wavy and wild as the wind channels between the hills and towards Kenmore.

DALERB

The favoured entry spot for local swimmers. There is an old sunken crannog around 400 metres to the right (south-west) of the entry point, marked with a small buoy, which you will find if you swim parallel to the shore. It is very shallow around it – a wee island, just beneath the surface. It makes a good turnaround point. Watch out for water skiers and pleasure boats in the summer.

KENMORE BEACH

This is the most obvious swimming location in Kenmore. It is very shallow for a long time, so you have to wade out for quite a way before you can swim properly. I've swum from here, out and around the wee island to the left. It is shallow but swimmable. Watch out for boats; tow floats are essential.

TAYMOUTH MARINA

A perfect spot for a quick winter dip or a longer swim when the water is warmer. Get in via the concrete slipway between the marina and the old crannog centre. From here, you can also swim to Kenmore or swim parallel to the shore in the other direction if the marina is quiet. Please note that this entry spot is right beside the entrance of a busy marina; when the marina is in use (usually from April to October) it is best to swim from here either early or late in the day.

TECHNICAL INFORMATION

DESCRIPTION **freshwater loch**   MAXIMUM DEPTH **155m**   LENGTH **23km**   MAXIMUM WIDTH **1.1km**
ELEVATION **105m**   GOOD FOR **stunning scenery; winter dips; longer summer swims**   LOCAL GROUP **Perthshire Wild Swimmers; Tayside Wild Swimmers**

Dalerb

ACCESS **close to car park; grassy track to the water**
ENTRY **very rocky; gets deep very quickly**
LOCATION **56.5814, -4.0187**

Kenmore Beach

ACCESS **close to car park; path to the beach**
ENTRY **stony; shallow for a long way out**
LOCATION **56.5839, -3.9973**

Taymouth Marina

ACCESS **short walk along road and path**
ENTRY **concrete slipway; deep enough to swim quickly**   LOCATION **56.5797, -4.0034**

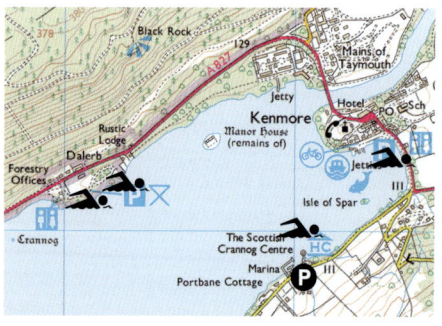

Getting there – Loch Tay

Loch Tay is on the A827 between Killin and Aberfeldy. The village of Kenmore is at the northern tip of the loch.

Getting there – Dalerb

From Kenmore, take the A827 along the northern shore of Loch Tay. Around 1.2 kilometres after the Drummond Hill turning, the car park entrance is on the left, opposite some steps coming down the hill. Parking is limited. Note that this is the new site of the Scottish Crannog Centre. There will likely be some disruption in the area while the building works are ongoing.

Getting there – Kenmore Beach

Just south of the main part of Kenmore village there is a small car park (parking charge; not suitable for large or high vehicles) next to the beach. However, there is alternative parking in a lay-by right opposite the beach.

Getting there – Taymouth Marina

Turn off the A827 on to the road which hugs Loch Tay's southern shore. After 600 metres, you will see the turning for Taymouth Marina car park on the left.

Notes

There are lots of speedboats on the loch during the summer – it is best to swim in the early morning or in the evening during this time. Tow floats are essential at all times.

If you fancy a treat, book yourself in for a session at the HotBox, Taymouth Marina's lochside spa. There is a huge sauna and a hot tub, with stunning views and access (via a slide or steps) to the loch.

1 Loch Tay, south side   2 Taymouth Marina ramp entry   3 Still water of Loch Tay © Vivien Cumming

Refreshments

» **The Courtyard Bar & Brasserie**, Kenmore. Large establishment with cosy fireplace. Good for food or post-swim hot drinks. Seasonal.

» **The Ferryman's Inn**, Taymouth Marina. Cosy restaurant on the banks of Loch Tay. Great pizzas.

» **Habitat Cafe**, Aberfeldy. Friendly cafe with great coffee and an exceptional cake selection. Lovely masala chai – my favourite!

Falls of Falloch

With its viewpoint looking over the impressive waterfall, the Falls of Falloch is a popular tourist destination and a stopping point on the A82. It is also known as Rob Roy's Bathtub as, according to legend, outlaw Rob Roy MacGregor used to bathe in the deep pool below the waterfall. It's unsurprising then that the large deep pool has become a popular dipping spot. Make sure you avoid visiting during peak holiday times as it can get extremely busy.

I have enjoyed some wonderful dips here. The water is surprisingly clear, and you can swim right up to the waterfall after prolonged dry spells. While the pool beneath the waterfall can be calm and inviting, I have also seen the river raging with incredible force. Do not swim after heavy rain, as river levels can rise quickly. River levels really do need to be low for you to consider swimming here.

THE SWIM

From the car park, follow the gravelly path parallel to the road for about 300 metres until you reach the viewpoint. Then, head down towards the river to a rocky area. I have found the best place to get in is at the point the river exits the pool, beneath the main viewpoint.

The entry is a bit tricky as you have to get into the river and over some rocks before you get into the pool. Make sure you have something grippy on your feet, as the rocks are very slippery. My tactic is to bum-slide across the rocks until I get into the pool, which is shallow at first but soon drops off and becomes very deep.

You might need to change quickly in the summer as there can be a lot of midges!

TECHNICAL INFORMATION

DESCRIPTION **waterfall pool**   RIVER **Falloch** ELEVATION **90m**   ACCESS **300m walk from the car park, then a steep, rocky section to get down to river**   ENTRY **rocky and slippery; protective footwear needed**   GOOD FOR **waterfall pool dip; early morning swims before the crowds arrive; easy access from the A82**   SEPA WATER LEVEL **Falloch @Glenfalloch: the levels really need to be 'low' (or just above) to safely swim here** LOCATION **56.3502, -4.6929**

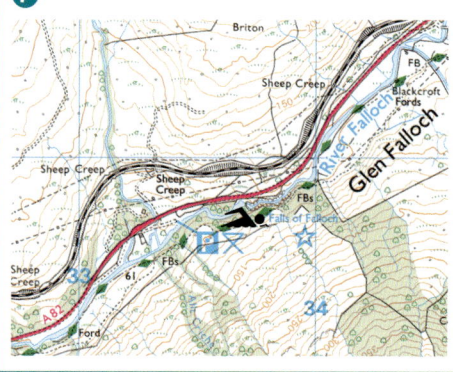

Getting there

The Falls of Falloch car park is seven kilometres south of Crianlarich on the A82. The car park is signed but easy to miss. There is limited parking, and the car park is not suitable for long vehicles as there isn't much room for turning. It is best to arrive early in the morning, before the crowds, if you want any chance of having the place to yourself.

Notes

Sadly, this location has become somewhat infamous in recent years, with countless water rescue incidents and horrible injuries, due to people leaping, diving or 'tombstoning' off the rocks into the pool below. While jumping into

1 Falls of Falloch

the water from a great height can be fun, *please don't do it*. This can be a wonderful place to swim if you are careful, have prior acclimation and get in gradually. This is also a warning that if you are there at a busy time, people may be attempting to jump in. Make sure you are not underneath them when they do!

Refreshments

» **The Drovers Inn**, Inverarnan. Just a few kilometres south on the A82. One of the oldest (and most haunted) pubs in Scotland, it's worth popping in for a post-swim meal, hot drink or pint.

» **Artisan Cafe & Deli**, Tyndrum. If you are heading north on the A82 towards Tyndrum, this is a great quirky cafe in an old, converted church. Fabulous home-made cakes.

» **The Real Food Cafe**, Tyndrum. The best gluten-free fish and chips in Scotland. Breakfasts and burgers also available. There is always a delicious selection of cakes on display too.

Loch Voil

Loch Voil is a hidden treasure in the Trossachs. It is a beautiful loch with spectacular views; my first experience dipping here was as part of a BBC *Countryfile* feature on winter swimming back in 2019. I was instantly blown away by the magnificent location and stunning reflections, and I always try and make an effort to swim here if I am travelling in this direction.

It isn't the easiest place to access in terms of parking, but that means it is much quieter than other local lochs. Make sure you pop into the Monachyle Mhor Hotel or Mhor 84 to warm up afterwards.

THE SWIM

The entry is pebbly and slopes off reasonably quickly from the beach. I've always just pootled around here and soaked up the glorious views, but I know others have done longer swims along the length of the loch. The water is very quiet, and you are unlikely to come across anyone apart from the occasional fisherman.

TECHNICAL INFORMATION

DESCRIPTION **freshwater loch** MAXIMUM DEPTH **30m** LENGTH **5.6km** MAXIMUM WIDTH **400m** ELEVATION **120m** ACCESS **500m walk from car park (includes stile) or cycle in from east end** ENTRY **pebbly beach** GOOD FOR **spectacular views; peaceful dips; longer swims** LOCATION **56.3439, -4.4628**

Getting there

Loch Voil is to the west of Strathyre and the A84. Turn off the A84 between Loch Lubnaig and Loch Earn, signposted *Balquhidder* and *Monachyle Mhor Hotel*. Follow the road under the bridge, carry on through Balquhidder village and then continue on for a further six kilometres along the edge of the loch until you get to the Monachyle Mhor Hotel. As tempting as it is, please don't park in the lay-bys along the way, as they mostly double up as passing places and the road can easily get blocked. Once you turn on to the hotel's driveway, park in the designated visitor parking area.

Alternatively, leave your car at the eastern end of the loch or at Mhor 84 and cycle along the narrow road until you get to a suitable entry spot.

Access

From the car park, walk down the drive and turn left on to the road and down the hill. Don't go through the first gate. Instead, cross the bridge and climb over the stile on the right immediately after the river. Watch out for barbed wire. Follow the track that takes you past the boat shed and curves round to the pebbly beach.

Please note that if the water levels are high, this area can flood and the beach will disappear underwater.

Refreshments

- » **Monachyle Mhor Hotel**, Balquhidder. Treat yourself to lunch or drinks at the beautiful hotel near the loch. Booking required.
- » **Mhor 84**, Balquhidder. Great selection of cakes, pastries, hot drinks and delicious meals.

Loch Lubnaig

Loch Lubnaig is a deep, narrow loch that snakes through the valley between Benvane and Ben Ledi to the west and Ben Vorlich to the east. The name Lubnaig comes from the Gaelic for 'elbow' or 'crooked', referring to the loch's bent shape. Being surrounded by high hills means that the loch is usually sheltered from the prevailing wind. Its proximity to the A84 means it has become a popular location for open water swimmers.

It is a perfect place to potter around and enjoy the views or to rack up the miles for some long-distance training. My longest swim here was an eight-hour training swim, doing lengths between the two car parks and being fed jelly babies and bananas every hour. The conditions were 'mixed' with moments of flat calm, followed by torrential rain and high winds. Honestly, the panini from The Cabin afterwards felt like the best I had ever tasted!

THE SWIM

Entering the loch, it is shallow for a few metres before shelving sharply, meaning that you are in deep water very quickly. To swim from the northern car park to the other side is just over 350 metres (one way). It is just over 1.1 kilometres (one way) between the two car parks.

In the middle of the loch, between the car parks, there is a submerged crannog which sometimes has two Scottish flags flying from it. This confused me the first time I swam here. I thought it was a paddleboarder, so I waved and said hello. It wasn't until I got back to the car park that I realised it was just a couple of flags.

This is a good loch for experienced swimmers rather than beginners (unless you are with a qualified lifeguard or swimming coach). If you are just starting out or are uncertain about swimming in deep water, nearby Loch Venachar (overleaf) is probably a better bet.

1 Loch Lubnaig © Anna Deacon   **2 The author setting off for another lap of Loch Lubnaig** © Sam Lyon
3 Loch Lubnaig © Anna Deacon   **4 Loch Venachar** © Shutterstock/Daniel Letford

There is not much boat traffic on the loch, except for the occasional canoe or small fishing boats, so it can be a tranquil spot for a swim, although it does get extremely busy during the school holidays.

TECHNICAL INFORMATION

DESCRIPTION **freshwater loch**   MAXIMUM DEPTH **45m**   LENGTH **6.4km**   MAXIMUM WIDTH **380m**   ELEVATION **120m**   ACCESS **right by the car parks**   ENTRY **gravel; steep drop into deep water**   GOOD FOR **more experienced swimmers; beautiful views; quick dips or long swims**   LOCAL GROUP **Wild West Swimmers; Lubnaig Loonies**   LOCATION **56.2774, -4.2841; 56.2671, -4.2856**

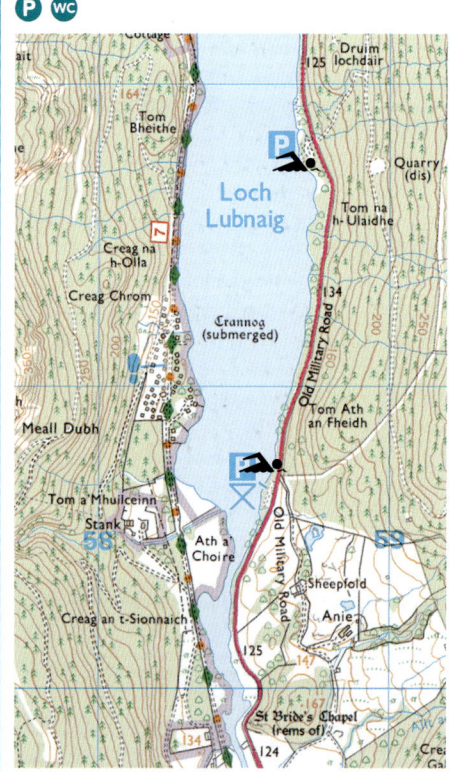

Getting there

Loch Lubnaig is right next to the A84, with Callander to the south and Strathyre to the north. There are two main car parks next to the loch, both pay and display and with limited opening hours. During school holidays the car parks can fill up very quickly, so it's best to get there early.

The northern car park has toilet facilities when The Cabin is open.

Refreshments

» **The Cabin**, A84, Loch Lubnaig. Right next to the loch, this is a great place for post-swim hot drinks and cake. Excellent (and very large) paninis. Takeaway only. Seasonal.

Alternatively, head to Callander for some other great options (see page 133).

Loch Venachar

Nestled in the hills, Loch Venachar is a beautiful, tree-lined loch close to Callander in the Trossachs. The views are glorious, especially on a calm day when the loch turns into a mirror. The name of the loch comes from Gaelic *Loch Bheannchair*, meaning 'horn-shaped loch'.

I find this a lovely, welcoming loch. It has a gently sloping entry, making it suitable for beginners as well as for experienced swimmers wanting to swim longer distances.

As with all swimming spots in the Trossachs, it can get busy in the summer. Thankfully, Loch Venachar is designated as a 'quiet loch' with a speed limit of four miles per hour for powerboats, meaning it is generally safe for swimming. However, you still need to be aware of other water users, and tow floats are essential.

NORTHERN SHORE

The swim east from the largest, westernmost car park to the pontoon at Venachar Lochside (a wedding venue) is almost exactly one kilometre. For shorter swims, it is around 250 metres between the two main car parks and 450 metres between the middle car park and the lay-by to the east.

SOUTHERN SHORE

This side of the loch is normally quieter than the northern side as it isn't so convenient to access from the main road. The entry is shallow and gently sloping. Footwear is recommended as it is a bit pebbly. You can swim in either direction parallel to the shore. Stay visible and be aware of the sailing club which can get busy in the summer months.

TECHNICAL INFORMATION

DESCRIPTION **freshwater loch**   MAXIMUM DEPTH **33m**   LENGTH **6km**   MAXIMUM WIDTH **970m**
ELEVATION **80m**   ACCESS **right by car parks**   ENTRY **stony; gradually sloping**   GOOD FOR **beginners or experienced swimmers; peaceful dips; beautiful views**   LOCAL GROUP **Wild West Swimmers**   LOCATION **Northern Shore 56.2264, -4.3236; 56.2261, -4.3195; 56.2261, -4.3123; Southern Shore 56.2223, -4.2725**

Northern Shore

Southern Shore

Getting there

Loch Venachar is between the town of Callander and the small settlement of Brig o' Turk, with the A821 running along its northern shore.

For the Northern Shore, there are several places to park just off the A821 towards the western end of the loch, including two car parks with picnic benches. There are no other facilities.

For the Southern Shore, turn off the A821 at the eastern end of the loch on to a minor road signposted *Invertrossachs*. Go over the bridge, turn right, and continue for two kilometres until you reach the car park. You can also reach the Southern Shore easily by bike, along Sustrans Route 7 from Callander.

Refreshments

» **Mhor Bread**, Callander. Amazing little bakery, shop and tearoom. Great pies, cakes and bread as well as tasty breakfasts and lunches.

» **Deli Ecosse**, Callander. Deli and cafe with delicious home-made cakes and scones.

Loch Lomond

I swam the length of Loch Lomond – north to south, from Ardlui to Balloch – in 2018. It's the third longest freshwater loch in Scotland (after Loch Awe and Loch Ness) but by far the largest in terms of surface area. It took me just over 14 hours to complete the swim, and I can confirm it is indeed a very long loch! End to end, it is further than swimming across the English Channel.

Loch Lomond has become a very popular place for open water swimming over the last few years, with many groups and individuals swimming in the loch year-round. It is also one of Scotland's most popular tourist hotspots and can get extremely busy over the summer months. During these times, you'll need to swim early in the morning or late in the day to find some peace and quiet.

Here's my pick of the locations on Loch Lomond – the first three are on the western shore (working south to north) and the last one is on the eastern shore.

DUCK BAY

If you swim parallel to the beach, you can easily stay within standing depth if you want to. Watch out for the semi-submerged posts if you swim to the right towards the hotel.

If you venture into deeper water, make sure you stay within the yellow-buoyed area. These are speed-restriction buoys for boat traffic, but sadly there is no guarantee that boats will pay attention to them. If you are lucky, you might see the seaplane taking off or landing while you swim.

LUSS

This is an incredibly popular swimming spot; if you swim in the morning, you will likely find other people swimming too. The beach and water can get very busy during peak times, so early or late swims are best to avoid the crowds and speedboats. There are speed restrictions on the shoreside of the yellow buoys, but sadly these are sometimes ignored. You must wear a tow float if you swim here, and stay away from the pier, as this is where the larger tourist boats come in and out.

For something more organised, Inchbaggers Loch Lomond hold a social swim on Sunday mornings; there is a charge for safety cover.

FIRKIN POINT

Only suitable for experienced swimmers. The drastic change in depth is only a few metres from the shore and so this spot is not advised for nervous or beginner swimmers. You will also notice the sudden drop in temperature as you hit the deeper water. Inexperienced swimmers should opt for Luss or Duck Bay, where the entries are more gradual.

The south bay tends to be nice and quiet even when the other beach is busy. There don't seem to be too many pleasure boats around this part of the loch but, to be safe, stick to the edge and wear a tow float.

MILARROCHY BAY

This is the best swimming spot I've found on the eastern side of Loch Lomond, although beware the dreaded midges in summer! I'm not sure why they are worse on this side of the loch, but they do seem to be. There are also usually fewer boats in this part of the loch, but always ensure that you are visible by wearing a tow float.

If you get in close to the car park and swim parallel to the shore, it is around 400 metres north (one way) to the end of the beach.

TECHNICAL INFORMATION

DESCRIPTION **freshwater loch**   MAXIMUM DEPTH **190m**   LENGTH **36km**   MAXIMUM WIDTH **8km**
ELEVATION **10m**   GOOD FOR **various entry points; beautiful views; short dips; longer swims**
LOCAL GROUP **Wild West Swimmers**   SEPA BATHING WATERS **water quality tested (at Luss) June–September**

Duck Bay

ACCESS **short walk from the car park; beach
access is just north of Duck Bay Hotel walls**
ENTRY **sandy; slightly gravelly; gently sloping**
LOCATION **56.0168, -4.6111**

Luss

ACCESS **short walk on a paved path to the beach**
ENTRY **sandy; slightly gravelly; gently sloping**
LOCATION **56.1033, -4.6378**

Firkin Point

ACCESS **short walk along a path to the beach**
ENTRY **gravel beach; steep, sudden drop off into
deep water**   LOCATION **56.1715, -4.6774**

Milarrochy Bay

ACCESS **short concrete ramp straight on to the
beach**   ENTRY **stony/gravelly; gently sloping entry;
it takes a while to get deep enough to swim**
LOCATION **56.0961, -4.5567**

Getting there – Loch Lomond

Loch Lomond is fairly easy to get to. Its southern
tip is around 34 kilometres from Glasgow. There
is a railway station in Balloch, with direct trains
to Glasgow. Buses will take you to some of
the places on Loch Lomond, particularly the
southern part of the western shore.

Getting there – Duck Bay

From Balloch, head north along the A82 for two
kilometres. Turn right, signposted *Duck Bay
Hotel*, and follow the road for a few hundred
metres and you'll see a car park on the left.

1 Loch Lomond shores © Shutterstock/Scott Clarence

Getting there – Luss

Luss is around 14 kilometres north of Balloch on the western side of the loch; it is well signed from the A82. There is a large pay-and-display car park.

Getting there – Firkin Point

The car park at Firkin Point has a prominent entrance off the A82, between Inverbeg and Tarbet. From the car park, head straight across the cycle path to the little track behind some signs, then either go straight ahead to the main beach or head right to reach the south bay.

Getting there – Milarrochy Bay

From Balloch, head east on the A811 towards Drymen. Heading towards the village, join the B858 and then the B837 to reach Balmaha. Around two kilometres past Balmaha, you will get to the entrances to the Milarrochy Bay car parks.

There are two small car parks with separate entrances and a wee bridge connecting them. The car park attendant will close the gate when the car park is full to prevent overcrowding. Thankfully the gates don't get shut at night, so early morning swims are possible.

Notes

There are lots of speedboats on the loch over the summer – the best swimming is in the early morning or in the evening during these months. Tow floats are essential at all times.

During extremely busy times, the road up the eastern side of Loch Lomond is closed by the police at the junction in Drymen to prevent unmanageable congestion along the narrow road.

Refreshments

» At Duck Bay, **Bobby's Cafe** inside Duck Bay Hotel is great for hot drinks and food.
» Bring your own food to Luss and cook at the barbecue benches. Alternatively, the cafe at the **Luss Village Shop** is excellent for post-swim coffee, cake or something more substantial (including some good vegan options). There is an additional snack bar in summer.
» There are lots of picnic benches at Firkin Point, which are great for bring-your-own post-swim snacks and hot drinks.
» For Milarrochy Bay, either bring a picnic or stop at **St Mocha Coffee Shop** in Balmaha. It has fantastic coffee and delicious cakes and food.

CENTRAL & SOUTHERN SCOTLAND

Opposite St Mary's Loch © Grahame Connor

Kingsbarns Beach

Kingsbarns Beach is a three-kilometre stretch of golden sands and rocky outcrops; it is protected from southwesterly winds, meaning it is often a sheltered place to swim. The last time I swam here, the sea was mirror flat, with only occasional ripples as the waves broke gently on the shore. Of course, if the wind is blowing from the east, there can be a bigger swell, but the offshore skerries give some protection from larger waves.

THE SWIM

There are a couple of places to swim. The first is the narrow sandy channel, near the car park, between the old wall and the giant rock pool. You can also dip in the rock pool, which can be pretty shallow and seaweedy, but creates a sheltered natural pool at low tide.

   If you walk slightly further south from the car park, you will find a larger sandy area known as Cambo Sands. The entry here is gently sloping and sandy, although there are a few submerged rocks. Swimming here at mid-to-high tide can be fantastic, but it is best to swim at low tide first so you know where the rocks are.

TECHNICAL INFORMATION

DESCRIPTION **beach**   ORIENTATION **north-east**
TIDES **possible to swim at any point in the tide; watch out for submerged rocks at mid-to-high tide**
ACCESS **steps down to the beach from the car park; 300m walk to Cambo Sands**   ENTRY **sand**
GOOD FOR **sunrise swims; rock pools; sheltered swims**   LOCAL GROUP **Fife Wild Swimmers**
SEPA BATHING WATERS **water quality tested June–September**   LOCATION **56.3027, -2.6425**

Getting there

The village of Kingsbarns is 11 kilometres east of St Andrews on the A917. From the village, turn on to Back Stile, signposted *Coastal Path Parking*. After one kilometre you get to the large beach car park. There is plenty of space, but it can fill up quickly on sunny weekends.

Alternatively, regular buses run between St Andrews and Leven, stopping at Kingsbarns.

Refreshments

» **The Cheesy Toast Shack**, Kingsbarns Beach car park. Handy snack and hot drink cabin right next to the beach. Great for gooey grilled-cheese sandwiches, hot dogs, cold drinks and hot chocolate. Seasonal.

» **Cambo Gardens Cafe**, Kingsbarns. Excellent vegetarian and vegan food. Great coffee and lovely gardens. Indoor and outdoor seating.

Fife Tidal Pools

There are three wonderful artificial tidal pools along the East Neuk of Fife coastline, at Pittenweem, St Monans and Cellardyke. All have been brought back to life and are up and running again thanks to the efforts of passionate and dedicated community members. Although you are swimming in sea water, these tidal pools are a safe haven – somewhere to swim, even when the weather is wild. Pittenweem is the deepest and is built 'end on' to the sea, whereas St Monans and Cellardyke pools are fairly shallow and built broadside to the sea. With them all being so close together, swimming in all three in a day is possible and would be a fantastic day out.

PITTENWEEM TIDAL POOL

Pittenweem is definitely my favourite of the Fife tidal pools. The seaward end feels like an infinity pool. Gazing over the edge towards North Berwick and looking out for whales and dolphins in the Firth of Forth is always exciting.

Records of a pool at this site date back to 1895. However, it was rebuilt and refurbished by locals after World War II to create the pool that we recognise today. In its heyday, the pool also had a diving board, a chute, a float in the middle, a cafe and a row of wooden changing cubicles. The pool was incredibly popular with families before it sadly fell out of use in the 1980s.

Thankfully, after years of campaigning to restore the pool to its former glory, the West Braes Project secured £270,000 of funding to renovate it. As a result, swimmers have been enjoying the pool since the summer of 2021.

While it is possible to swim here any time, mid-to-low tide is perfect. The pool is less sheltered at high tide, as the walls can be submerged meaning waves break over the edge. The pool has clear water and a sandy beach entry, but still wear something to protect your feet as there are a few stones underfoot.

Pittenweem is deeper at the far end (around two metres) than any of the other local tidal pools, which means it feels like somewhere you can have a proper swim rather than just a shallow paddle. Swimming here on sunny days, I really struggle to persuade myself to get out, always thinking, 'just one more lap!'

ST MONANS TIDAL POOL

A gorgeous pool overlooked by a windmill that once pumped sea water to the nearby long-abandoned salt pans, St Monans tidal pool has also been brought back to life by local volunteers after 40 years of neglect. In February 2021 a clearing party extracted dangerous hazards, including glass, rocks and rusting metal, making the pool swimmable again.

Although the pool is now periodically drained and cleared by volunteers it is not officially maintained. The access is down steep stone steps and is quite stony underfoot, so foot protection is recommended.

CELLARDYKE TIDAL POOL

Cellardyke's pool, known as 'The Bathie', was built in the early 1930s and was hugely popular for many years until it fell out of use in the late 1970s. In the last few years locals worked hard to clear the pool of rocks, seaweed and debris and in 2021 the community group received funding to continue renovations. There are new steps to allow better access down to the area, colourful hooks to hang your kit up and a ladder to get into the pool.

It is now a bustling place in the summer, with a play park, coffee trailer and activities offered by East Neuk Outdoors. Get in down the new steps and swim widths or paddle in the shallows at the southern end.

TECHNICAL INFORMATION

Pittenweem Tidal Pool

DESCRIPTION **tidal pool**   ORIENTATION **southwest**   LENGTH **75m (50m swimmable)**   WIDTH **25m**   MAXIMUM DEPTH **2m**   TIDES **best at mid-to-low tide; possible at high tide but the walls will be submerged**   ACCESS **120m walk from car park; steep steps down to the changing area and pool**   ENTRY **sand with a few rocks**   GOOD FOR **sheltered swims; leisurely lengths; wildlife spotting**   LOCAL GROUPS **Pittenweem Menopausal Mermaids; Wild Skins**   LOCATION **56.2105, -2.7377**

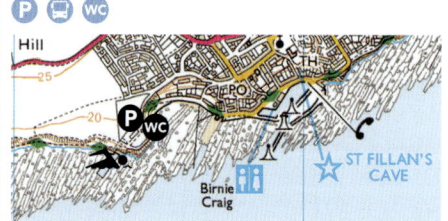

St Monans Tidal Pool

DESCRIPTION **tidal pool**   ORIENTATION **south**   LENGTH **100m (75m swimmable)**   WIDTH **25m**   MAXIMUM DEPTH **2m**   TIDES **best at mid-to-low tide; possible at high tide but the walls will be submerged**   ACCESS **400m walk along coastal path from car park; steep steps down to pool**   ENTRY **stony (can be slippery); protective footwear essential**   GOOD FOR **leisurely lengths; sheltered swims**   LOCAL GROUPS **Wild Skins**   LOCATION **56.2062, -2.7550**

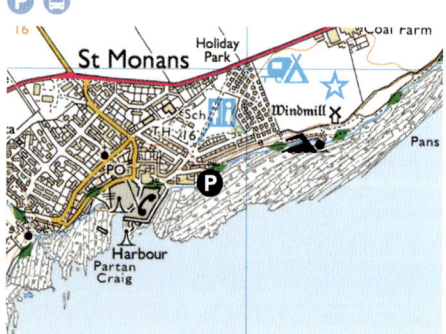

Cellardyke Tidal Pool

DESCRIPTION **tidal pool**   ORIENTATION **southeast**   LENGTH **150m (100m swimmable but still quite shallow)**   WIDTH **25m**   MAXIMUM DEPTH **2m**   TIDES **best at mid-to-low tide; possible at high tide but the walls will be submerged**   ACCESS **short walk to the pool; metal steps down to pool**   ENTRY **via a ladder or walk in at the shallow end (can be slippery); protective footwear recommended**   GOOD FOR **leisurely lengths; kids paddling; sheltered swims**   LOCAL GROUPS **Wild Skins; Cellardyke Tidal Pool**   LOCATION **56.2274, -2.6805**

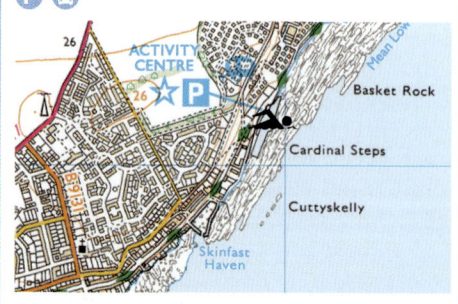

Getting there – Pittenweem Tidal Pool

From the A917 in Pittenweem, follow the signs for *Coastal Path Parking*. There is a large car park (and overflow parking) with a toilet block. Alternatively, regular buses run between St Andrews and Leven, stopping at Pittenweem.

Getting there – St Monans Tidal Pool

Leave the A917 and park in the small car park at the end of Rose Street. Walk along the Fife Coastal Path to reach the pool. Alternatively, regular buses run between St Andrews and Leven, stopping at St Monans.

Getting there – Cellardyke Tidal Pool

Leave the A917 and park in the small car park on East End, which is next to the pool. Alternatively, regular buses run between St Andrews and Leven, stopping at Cellardyke.

Refreshments

» **Cocoa Tree Cafe**, Pittenweem. A choco-holic's paradise with luxurious hot chocolates and chocolate cake. Also, artisan coffee, speciality teas, and a range of soups and sandwiches, so there is something for everyone (even if you don't like chocolate). Great gluten-free and dairy-free options.

» **Giddy Gannet**, St Monans. Lovely little cafe with fantastic coffee and an amazing cake selection (I recommend the carrot cake). The sausage rolls are pretty awesome too!

» **The Grind**, Cellardyke. Coffee, crepes, toasties and other tasty things, served from a shiny Airstream trailer right by the pool. Everything is delicious.

Kinghorn Harbour Beach

Overlooking the Firth of Forth, Kinghorn's Harbour Beach is a popular place to swim for locals and visitors alike. Access via public transport is very convenient: Kinghorn railway station is only a short walk from the beach.

The beach is just a narrow strip of sand at high tide, with the harbour on one side and the RNLI lifeboat station on the other. The station is known to be one of the busiest in Scotland, covering the south Fife coastline and parts of Edinburgh. At low tide, the beach turns into a vast expanse of sand, backed by towering cliffs and rock pools.

THE SWIM

Kinghorn is an excellent place for swimming as the shallow-sloping beach allows you to stay easily within your depth. Locals tend to favour swimming at high tide as the water is closer and gets deeper quite quickly. There is a long way to walk to the water at low tide, and you have to wade out quite a way before it is deep enough to swim.

Kinghorn Sea Swimmers is a lovely, welcoming community of swimmers who swim at Kinghorn regularly. Please be mindful that access to the RNLI lifeboat station must be kept clear at all times. Several private houses also require access, and swimmers should respect the residents' privacy.

1 Kinghorn Harbour Beach © Shutterstock/Roy Henderson

TECHNICAL INFORMATION

DESCRIPTION **beach** ORIENTATION **south-east** TIDES **safe to swim at any time** ACCESS **steps and ramp down to beach** ENTRY **sandy, gently sloping; a bit pebbly at high tide** GOOD FOR **sunrise swims; refreshing dips** LOCAL GROUP **Kinghorn Sea Swimmers** SEPA BATHING WATERS **water quality tested June–September** LOCATION **56.0684, -3.1736**

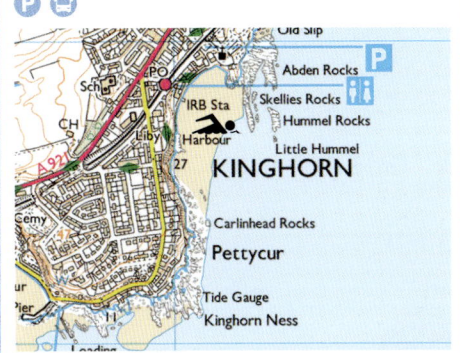

Getting there

Kinghorn is on the A921 between Burntisland and Kirkcaldy. There is a small car park on Harbour Road, but also some other options in the town. Kinghorn is well connected via public transport with good bus and rail links. There is a direct train link to Kinghorn from Edinburgh, Perth and Dundee, and it is a short walk down from the railway station to the beach, making it a great option if you want to escape to the sea.

Refreshments

» **Kinghorn Community Centre Cafe**, Kinghorn. Community cafe serving simple food and hot drinks.
» **Up She Pops**, Kinghorn. Cute little craft shop and cafe with friendly service – the perfect place for post-swim coffee and cake.
» **The Harbour View**, Kinghorn. Great views over the beach and harbour. Tasty food. Indoor and outdoor seating.

1 Seacliff Beach © Jane Sendall   **2** Looking across to Bass Rock from Seacliff Beach © Anna Deacon

Seacliff Beach

This corner of Scotland is a genuine hidden gem, with many fabulous beaches for swimming. My favourite is Seacliff Beach, with its spectacular views west to Tantallon Castle and north over the mighty Bass Rock. Situated only two kilometres offshore, this massive chunk of Carboniferous rock is home to the largest northern gannet colony in the world in peak breeding season.

Protected by cliffs and rocky outcrops from all but northerly winds, this is often a sheltered and peaceful place to swim. When the conditions are calm, the water is crystal clear, and it's worth dipping your face beneath the surface to look out for crabs scuttling along the sand, tiny fish and bright green seaweed.

THE SWIM

The beach entry is sandy and gently sloping. If you swim parallel to the shore, it's just over 400 metres to swim across the bay.

I've enjoyed swims here at high and low tide. Low tide offers the most sheltered conditions if the wind is coming from the east. If the tide is high, it's a shorter walk out to the water. Watch out for the submerged rocks at the edges and centre of the beach.

TECHNICAL INFORMATION

Getting there

If you've never been to Seacliff Beach before, it can be difficult to find, as the turning off the A198 is not well signposted. The beach is around six kilometres east of North Berwick. Turn off the A198 at Auldhame (where there is a right-angled bend in the road) on to a private estate road. Follow this, and soon you will see signs down to the beach. Turn left on to a rougher track and follow along to the first car park overlooking the beach. This parking area is pretty small and can be muddy. There are steep steps down to the beach.

If you carry on for another 300 metres, you will get to a larger car park with a grassy parking area and toilets. From here, it is a 50-metre walk along a sandy track to the beach.

Please note that the beach car parks are privately owned, and there is a coin-operated barrier to access them. The barriers are often shut at sunset, and there is no overnight parking.

Refreshments

» **Drift**, Canty Bay, North Berwick. Cafe made of shipping containers with spectacular views over the sea. Sit-in cafe and takeaway trailer. Amazing, locally sourced food.
» There are also multiple options in North Berwick, including **Steampunk Coffee** – a great place for coffee and cake – and **Bostock Bakery** – a brilliant little bakery and cafe with good coffee and delicious pastries.

DESCRIPTION **beach**   ORIENTATION **north**
TIDES **can swim at any time**   ACCESS **steps or 50m sandy path to beach**   ENTRY **sand**   GOOD FOR **fantastic views; sheltered swims; longer swims across the bay**   LOCAL GROUP **Bass Rock Swimmers; Wild Swimming – Edinburgh and Lothians**
SEPA BATHING WATERS **water quality tested June–September**   LOCATION **56.0525, -2.6350**

Ⓟ ⓦⓒ

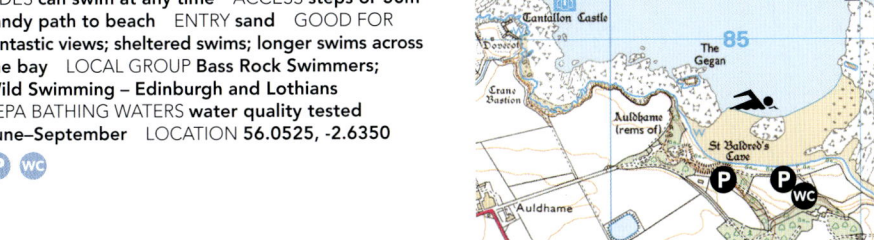

1 Underwater sunbeams, Seamill Beach   2 Ripples in the sand, Seamill Beach
3 Jumping for joy, Seamill Beach © Kiara Henderson

Seamill Beach

Seamill Beach is easy to access and has become popular with year-round swimmers and dippers. If it's not too cloudy, it has spectacular views across to Arran and down the Firth of Clyde. The first time I swam here, I was surprised at how clear the water was. I could see crabs scuttling along the sand, and the sunbeams glistened. I've also swum here on other days when the weather hasn't been so good, but I've always found the water inviting. Watch for whales and dolphins out at sea.

THE SWIM

There is an area of rocks opposite the car park (submerged at low tide) that break the beach into two sections. The entry is sandy and gently sloping on each side of the rocks, but there are some seaweedy patches, particularly at low tide. There are a few submerged rocks at the northern end of the beach.

If you want a longer swim and the conditions allow, the northern section of the beach is just over 400 metres long, and the southern section is around 200 metres long.

4 Sunset splash, Seamill Beach © Kiara Henderson

TECHNICAL INFORMATION

DESCRIPTION **beach**   ORIENTATION **south-west**
TIDES **can swim at any time**   ACCESS **car park
right by the beach**   ENTRY **sand**   GOOD FOR
**sunset swims; views of Arran; longer swims along
the bay**   LOCAL GROUP **Wild Sea Women –
Ayrshire**   SEPA BATHING WATERS **water quality
tested June–September**   LOCATION **55.6860,
-4.8678**

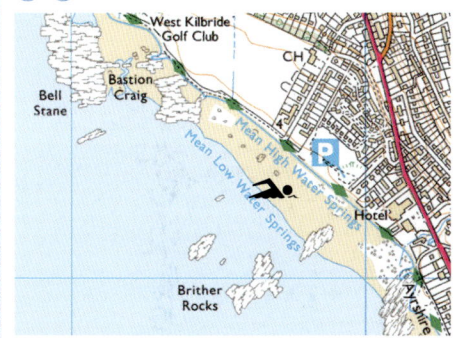

Getting there

Seamill Beach is situated near West Kilbride,
on the A78 between Largs and Ardrossan.
There are good bus connections to local towns,
and there is a railway station in nearby West
Kilbride. If you're arriving by car, there is a large
car park with a height barrier and direct access
to the beach.

Refreshments

» **The View**, Seamill House Hotel, Seamill.
Hotel restaurant with an amazing view.
Quite smart but close to the beach and
good for hot drinks and lunch.
» **POD**, West Kilbride. Lovely little cafe with
an excellent selection of cakes and hot
drinks. The breakfast pancake stacks are
highly recommended!
» **Curious Larder**, West Kilbride. Excellent
little deli and takeaway with fantastic cakes,
mini pies and sausage rolls. Pick something
up to munch on the beach post-swim.

Culzean Castle

The coastline around Culzean Castle is made up of a series of sandy bays interspersed with towering cliffs and lots of options for swimming.

MAIDENS BEACH

My favourite place for longer swims is Maidens Beach, which runs south from the forested Culzean Country Park to the holiday village of Maidens. Across the water lies Ailsa Craig and, on a clear day, you can even see across to the Mull of Kintyre.

The beach is long and sandy with some rocky patches. The best entry point is around 200 metres to the north of the northern car park, near a small burn. Here it is less stony and mainly sandy underfoot. It's around one kilometre to the rocks at the northern end of the beach from here.

PORT CARRICK BEACH

This hidden gem lies just north of Maidens Beach – a small but perfectly formed sandy lagoon tucked below Culzean Castle. Look out for wildlife, including seals, sea urchins and starfish. There have even been rumours of seahorses around this coastline, so keep your eyes peeled!

Port Carrick Beach is much smaller than Maidens Beach – only around 100 metres across – with a sandy, gently sloping entry. An hour or so after high tide Glasson Rock appears, protecting the beach to the west. The beach turns into a shallow, sandy lagoon, providing a sheltered place to swim without going out of your depth.

TECHNICAL INFORMATION

Maidens Beach

DESCRIPTION **beach**   ORIENTATION **west**
TIDES **best at high tide**   ACCESS **swim close to the road or walk 800m up the beach**
ENTRY **sandy with stony sections**   GOOD FOR **sunset swims; longer swims**   SEPA BATHING WATERS **water quality tested June–September**
LOCATION **55.3394, -4.8110**

Port Carrick Beach

DESCRIPTION **beach**   ORIENTATION **north-west**
TIDES **best an hour or so after high tide**
ACCESS **1.5km walk from Maidens (500m from Swan Pond) with steep steps down to beach**
ENTRY **sandy with stony sections**   GOOD FOR **sheltered swims in the lagoon**   LOCATION **55.3486, -4.8075**

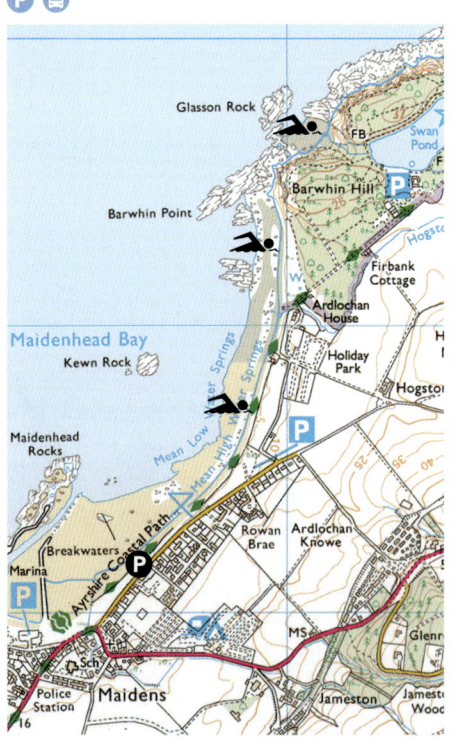

1 Maidens Beach

Getting there

Maidens is on the A719 between Ayr and Girvan. Once you get to Maidens turn on to Ardlochan Road, and the first seafront parking area is on your left after 250 metres. It's a further 250 metres up to the northern car park, where there are some Portaloos. Regular buses run between Ayr and Girvan, stopping at Maidens.

There is alternative parking for Port Carrick Beach at Swan Pond on the Culzean estate. You have to pay for parking here unless you are a National Trust for Scotland member.

Access

It is a short walk from the car parks in Maidens to the beach. If you want to find some peace and quiet, walk around 800 metres north up the beach. When you reach a small burn, turn right and cross the footbridge before heading back to the beach. This section of the bay is backed by woodland and has a very different feel from the southern section of the beach.

If you are happy to walk further, instead of sticking to Maidens Beach, take another right after the footbridge to follow small paths through the woods to reach Port Carrick Beach. There are steep steps down to the beach.

Refreshments

» **Little K's Kitchen**, Maidens. Local shop and cafe with a simple menu. Great hot drinks and food.
» **Ropes**, Maidens. Cafe and bistro with a view over the bay. Great for coffee and cake or a warming bowl of soup after your swim.

Loch Doon

Nestled in the Galloway Hills, Loch Doon is surrounded by rivers, mountains, forests and moors. It feels remote and rugged and can be exposed to the wind.

Although it is a great place to swim, it is also essential that you stay away from the dam at the northern end of the loch. Loch Doon is one of several storage reservoirs for Scottish Power's Galloway hydroelectric project. In 1935, a dam was erected at the northern end of the loch as part of the scheme's development. As a result, the loch's water level rose by around ten metres, submerging an entire airbase that had been built on the edge of the loch 20 years earlier.

THE SWIM

At the northern end of the loch, there is a grassy track down to a stony beach. The entry is quite rough, so foot protection is essential. It gets deep very quickly. Ensure that you stay away from the dam. From the stony beach, swim to the right along the shore (heading south, parallel to the road), away from the dam.

The orientation of the loch means that the prevailing wind is channelled between the hills, and the water can become rough in the middle. The wind can easily carry you further down the loch and make it difficult to get back to your exit point. Do not swim across the loch at this point or into the narrow section close to the dam. The narrowing increases the strength of the current as water is drawn towards the dam.

At the southern end of the loch near the castle there is a grassy track with rocky sections leading to a sandy beach, as long as the water level isn't too high. The entry is gently sloping and becomes more gravelly as you go out, with a few larger stones. Stay within the bay and don't try to swim out to the island as the wind can blow you off course leaving you much further to swim back.

TECHNICAL INFORMATION

DESCRIPTION **freshwater loch**   MAXIMUM
DEPTH **30m**   LENGTH **9km**   MAXIMUM WIDTH
1.6km   ELEVATION **210m**   ACCESS **short walk;
grassy track with rocky sections**   ENTRY **rocky
and gets deep quickly; sandy beach at southern
end of the loch**   GOOD FOR **short dips; wildlife
spotting; swims along the shore**   LOCAL GROUP
The SouWesters   LOCATION **55.2811, -4.3988;
55.2247, -4.3839**   AVOID **the dam (55.2834,
-4.3991); hydro extraction point (55.2480, -4.3580)**

Getting there

Loch Doon is around six kilometres south of
Dalmellington. Turn off the A713 on to an
unclassified road, signposted *Loch Doon*.
The best parking for the northern end of
the loch is the lay-by immediately after the
Roundhouse cafe. At the southern end of
the loch there is a car park by the castle.

Safety note

Avoid the area around the dam at the northern
end of the loch. Also, there is an additional
extraction point for a hydroelectric scheme
approximately halfway down on the eastern
shore – avoid this area as it will also have
dangerous currents.

Refreshments

» **Roundhouse**, Loch Doon. Great little cafe
for post-swim hot drinks and snacks. Also
has an osprey viewing camera, so you
might be lucky enough to spot them on
the nest in the summer. Seasonal.

St Mary's Loch & Loch of the Lowes

With its stunning landscape of rounded hills,
deep valleys and views along the Yarrow Valley,
St Mary's Loch is the largest natural stretch of
water in the Borders. Although easily accessible,
the loch has a remote feel and is a beautiful
place to swim.

Immediately upstream of St Mary's Loch and
connected via a narrow channel is the smaller
Loch of the Lowes. With only 200 metres of
land separating the two lochs, and a car park
in the middle, it can be a good idea to choose
whichever body of water is most protected from
the wind on arrival.

THE SWIM

All the entry points to the lochs are stony.
Loch of the Lowes has a gently sloping incline
for a few metres before dropping away into
deeper water. The water is beautifully clean
and refreshing, and the view from the water is
wonderful. The loch is just over one kilometre
long, so it can also be suitable for longer swims.

St Mary's Loch is around 450 metres wide
at the southern end. In the summer it is best
to avoid the sailing club as it can be busy with
boats. This is a popular loch for long-distance
swimming training, with swimmers completing
the five-kilometre length of the loch in the
summer to train for long-distance events.

TECHNICAL INFORMATION

St Mary's Loch
MAXIMUM DEPTH **47m**   LENGTH **5km**
MAXIMUM WIDTH **800m**   ELEVATION **250m**
LOCATION **55.4737, -3.2063**

Loch of the Lowes
MAXIMUM DEPTH **18m**   LENGTH **1.2km**
MAXIMUM WIDTH **300m**   ELEVATION **250m**
LOCATION **55.4708, -3.2066**

DESCRIPTION **freshwater lochs**   ACCESS **easy
access from car park, or short walk to sailing club**
ENTRY **gravelly/stony**   GOOD FOR **scenic swims;
double dipping; longer swims in St Mary's Loch**
LOCAL GROUP **Wild Swimming Moffat;
Wild Swimming Borders; The SouWesters**

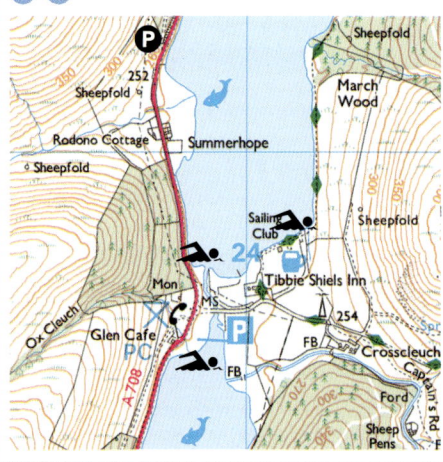

Getting there
Both lochs run alongside the A708 between
Moffat and Selkirk. The main parking area is in
the middle of the two lochs; there are toilets
and a cafe directly opposite. This area can get
pretty busy in the summer as it is a popular
paddleboarding, kayaking and camping spot.
There are multiple other lay-bys with space for
a couple of cars and entry points for St Mary's
Loch along the A708. I've swum from one just
under one kilometre north of the main car park.

Access
The central car park is only around 30 metres
from the shore of Loch of the Lowes. The closest
access to St Mary's Loch is 200 metres north of
the parking area.

   The sailing club is closed in winter, making
it a popular entry point for local swimmers.
From the central car park, walk along the lane,
go over the bridge and turn left. The gate will
be locked (no vehicle access), but you can walk
along to the clubhouse.

   Access from the lay-by parking is short and
steep, taking you down to a shingly beach as
long as the water levels are low enough.

Refreshments
» **Glen Cafe**, St Mary's Loch. Right opposite
the car park, this cafe is great for post-swim
bacon butties and coffee.

153

Loch Ettrick

Loch Ettrick is a small, peaceful loch in the heart of the Forest of Ae. It is a quiet place (until the noisy swimmers arrive!) where sound is dampened by the surrounding trees. At under 500 metres long, I find it a welcoming place to swim, sheltered by the surrounding woodland. The last time I swam here, it was flat calm, even though it was a windy day. Listen out for frogs croaking along the banks in the spring. A layer of ice can often cover the loch in the winter.

THE SWIM

There is an obvious entry point to the loch just next to the parking area. The grassy slope can be slippery and the entry a little muddy, so ensure you have something protective on your feet. Alternatively, you can walk down to the far side to get in. It's a shallow, gently sloping, grassy entry.

The earth embankment dam is around 230 metres long and, from the entry by the parking, it is about 150 metres along the dam wall to the bend. Watch out for weeds and water lilies near the boathouse. It's around 330 metres from the car park to the eastern end of the loch.

Loch Ettrick is colder than many other Dumfries and Galloway lochs, and the weather can change quickly and get very misty. However, the loch is generally sheltered and the waves never get very big due to the short length (fetch) of the loch. It can, however, change from mirror flat to choppy in minutes.

TECHNICAL INFORMATION

DESCRIPTION **freshwater loch** AVERAGE DEPTH **5m** LENGTH **490m** MAXIMUM WIDTH **200m** ELEVATION **270m** ACCESS **park by the loch; slippery after rain** ENTRY **grass; can be muddy underfoot** GOOD FOR **shorter swims; sheltered dips; colder water** LOCATION **55.2257, -3.6601**

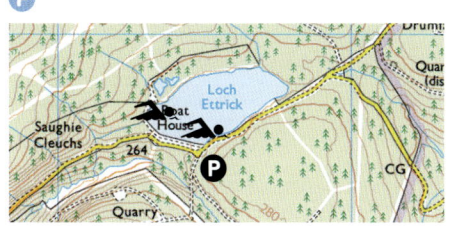

Getting there

Loch Ettrick is signed off the A76 just south of Closeburn. The road to the loch is narrow and single-track (with passing places); be aware that there can sometimes be forestry lorries using it.

There is a small parking area by a gate towards the western end of the loch. There is additional parking opposite, but make sure you don't block the forestry gate.

Safety note

An overflow pipe at the northern end of the dam discharges to a ditch leading to the outlet burn. Make sure you avoid this area. There can sometimes be blue–green algae at this loch in the summer.

Refreshments

Take a flask. There isn't anything close by, but there are a few options in nearby Thornhill.

» **Thomas Tosh**, Thornhill. Cafe and shop based in Thornhill's old parish hall. Delicious food and hot drinks.
» **Marchbank Bakers**, Thornhill. Good coffee, great cake, pastries, pies and filled rolls.

Loch Ken

Loch Ken is a long, narrow stretch of water popular with open water swimmers. It is part of a hydroelectric scheme, meaning that the water level fluctuates quite a lot and it is regularly filled with freshwater from the Galloway Hills.

The open water and wetlands of Loch Ken and the River Dee form the largest freshwater body in southern Scotland and are home to some fantastic wildlife. The wetlands around the south-western part of the loch are part of the RSPB's Ken-Dee Marshes Nature Reserve. Look out for great crested grebes, red kites and otters.

Other parts of the loch can get busy with boats; they have speed restrictions and there is a designated water ski zone. It's best to go early morning or later in the day during the summer months or go to one of the organised swims at Crossmichael Marina.

These swimming spots are ordered from south to north on the loch.

CROSSMICHAEL MARINA

A friendly little marina tucked down a quiet lane, popular with local swimmers who like to swim from the concrete slipway around the buoys and moored boats. There are regular group swims run by local swimming groups at Crossmichael Marina. Safety cover is provided, but swimmers are responsible for their own safety. Wear a bright hat and tow float. Anyone is welcome to join; a small cash contribution is required to help cover the cost of the safety boat.

As it can be a busy little marina, if you wish to swim here not as part of an organised group, it is advisable to tell one of the boatmen and make sure they are aware that you are swimming.

RAILWAY BRIDGE

This is a lovely place to swim from and a popular point for launching kayaks, canoes and paddleboards. You must stay clear of the water ski zone, which begins around 500 metres north of this entry spot.

GALLOWAY ACTIVITY CENTRE

Galloway Activity Centre hosts the annual Loch Ken Wild Swim event in September, and is generally welcoming to swimmers outside of its busy times. It is best to swim before 8 a.m. or after 4 p.m. to avoid getting in the way of any of its water-based activities.

Enter the water in front of the cafe and clubhouse building, just north of the main access pontoon. From this entry point, it is approximately 600 metres (one way) to the far side of the loch. Make sure you warm up with a post-swim visit to the Waterfront Cafe.

WESTERN SHORE

The water is metres from the car park and the entry stony, but it gets deep enough to swim fairly quickly. As an added bonus, it is lovely and peaceful on this side of the loch.

TECHNICAL INFORMATION

DESCRIPTION **freshwater loch** MAXIMUM DEPTH **18m** LENGTH **14km** MAXIMUM WIDTH **800m** ELEVATION **50m** ACCESS **easy – close to parking** ENTRY **gravel** GOOD FOR **easy access; organised swims at Crossmichael; beautiful scenery** LOCAL GROUP **Dumfries and Galloway Wild Swimmers; The SouWesters** LOCATION **Crossmichael Marina 54.9796, -3.9879; Railway Bridge 55.0101, -4.0585; Galloway Activity Centre 55.0375, -4.1021; Western Shore 55.0441, -4.1206** AVOID **water ski zone (55.01289, -4.0631 to 55.0293, -4.0911)**

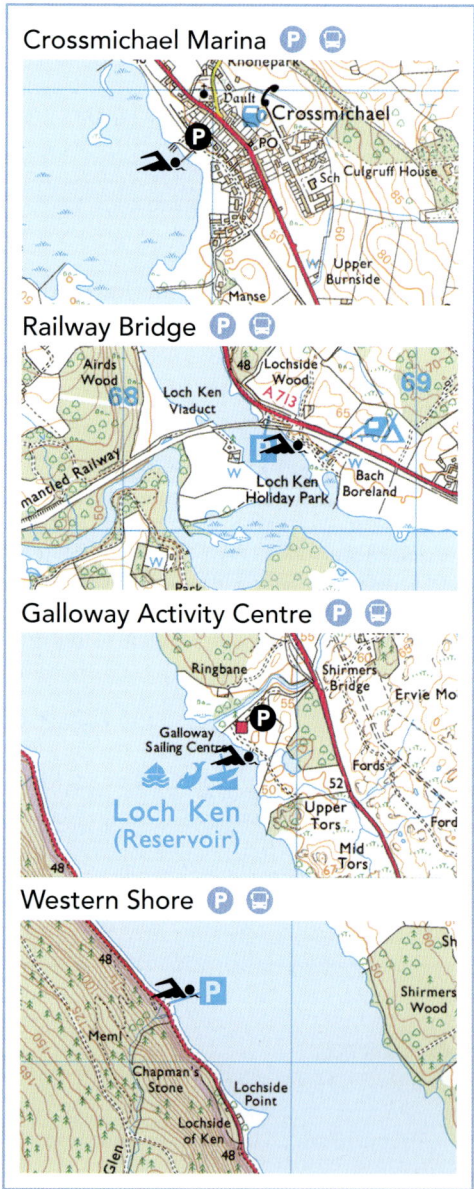

1 Loch Ken © Shutterstock/Richard P Long

Getting there – Crossmichael Marina

Crossmichael village is on the eastern shore of Loch Ken. The marina is along Riverside Lane; there is a car park between the houses and the marina. Park with your car boot towards the water – this means that the people in the houses overlooking the marina won't inadvertently spot you getting changed! There are no toilets or other facilities here.

Alternatively, regular buses run between Castle Douglas and Dalmellington, stopping at Crossmichael. It is a short walk down to the marina.

Getting there – Railway Bridge

There is a large lay-by to the west of Parton, approximately halfway along the eastern side of the loch. The lay-by shares one of its entrances with Loch Ken Holiday Park. Head through the railway underpass to the slipway on to the loch.

Getting there – Galloway Activity Centre

Galloway Activity Centre is towards the northern end of Loch Ken and has a well-signed entrance from the A713. The main parking is around 300 metres down the track. Once you get there, you need to walk through the gate and past the buildings towards the loch.

Getting there – Western Shore

There are a couple of lovely spots on the western side of the loch where you can park and enter the loch. My preferred entry spot is around four kilometres south of New Galloway on the A762.

Refreshments

» **Thistle Inn**, Crossmichael. Cosy pub close to Crossmichael Marina. Good food and home-made cakes.
» **Waterfront Cafe**, Galloway Activity Centre. The clubhouse at the activity centre is a great place for post-swim hot drinks and light bites. Wonderful views over the loch.
» **The Smithy**, New Galloway. Great little cafe with yummy food and an excellent selection of cakes.

Carrick Beach

Carrick Beach is a beautiful off-the-beaten-track swim spot along the Solway Coast. It is a magical place to swim as long as you get the tides right.

The beach is protected from the prevailing wind by the Islands of Fleet. Directly opposite the beach is the largest island, Ardwall Isle (or *Ard Bhaile*, meaning 'High Town'). At low tide there is hardly any water in the bay and you can walk all the way across to Ardwall Isle. It is one of 17 tidal islands that can be walked to from the Scottish mainland.

THE SWIM

The beach is a mixture of pebbles and sand. The entry is normally pebbly at high tide, with the sand only exposed at low-to-mid tide. There are some rocks at the side of the beach, which can be submerged at high tide.

It is only around 350 metres across to the island at mid-to-high tide, but there can be very strong sideways currents around the rocks and islands; it is best to swim at slack tide, ideally an hour before high tide, to avoid these.

TECHNICAL INFORMATION

Getting there

Although it is possible to approach the beach from the north via a narrow, bumpy track, it is preferable to approach from the east via Knockbrex. From the A75 follow signs to Borgue; Carrick is signed from the village. Turn left at Knockbrex and continue for one kilometre past Knockbrex Castle. There may be a closed livestock gate along this road. If so, make sure you close it behind you.

The road takes you all the way to the car park, although it gets rough as you approach the beach. The parking area is grassy and can be a bit muddy. There are no facilities.

Note that this is information for Carrick Beach. Slightly confusingly, there is another beach just to the north known as Carrick Bay or Carrick Shore. Some people do also swim there.

Refreshments

Bring a post-swim picnic or stop on the way home.

» **Cream o' Galloway**, Rainton. Famous for its ice cream, but also has a cafe for lunch and hot drinks. Can get very busy in the school holidays.
» **The Crafty Crow**, Gatehouse of Fleet. Excellent cafe, which is also a craft and fabric shop.
» **Mulberries**, Kirkcudbright. Great selection of cakes and bakes.
» **Moore's Fish & Chips**, Castle Douglas. Award-winning fish and chips.

DESCRIPTION **beach**   ORIENTATION **south-west**
TIDES **best an hour before high tide; too shallow
to swim at low tide**   ACCESS **car park above
beach; grassy slope to shore**   ENTRY **pebbly/
sandy**   GOOD FOR **sheltered swims; beautiful
views; seal spotting**   LOCAL GROUP **Dumfries
and Galloway Wild Swimmers**   SEPA BATHING
WATERS **water quality tested June–September**
LOCATION **54.8252, -4.2182**

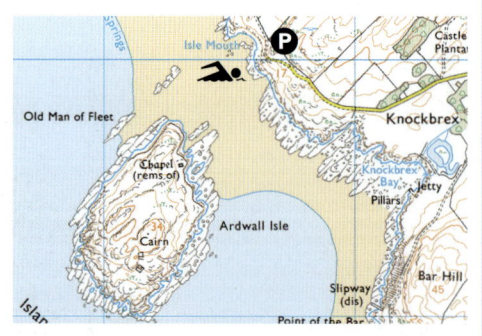

Acknowledgements

Writing this book has been a joy and a privilege – an opportunity to explore the amazing variety of swim locations around Scotland's mainland and islands, research new places to swim and revisit familiar spots, and – once pandemic restrictions were lifted – meet wonderful swimmers who generously shared their favourite local swim locations with me, along with considerable knowledge and enthusiasm.

Special thanks go to the Cairngorm Wild Swimmers, Loch Insh Dippers, Tiree Polar Bears, Orkney Polar Bears, Selkies – Shetland Open Water Swimming, Banffshire Coast Swimmers, Aberdeenshire Open Water Swimming, Ewe Wild Swimmers, Wild Highlanders, Hebridean Sea Swimmers, Lochaber Loons, Loch Leven (Glencoe) Wild Swimmers, Wild Swimming Borders, Wild West Swimmers and Fife Wild Swimmers.

Thank you to Vivien Cumming for her wonderful photography and to everyone else who contributed photographs to this book: Alastair Goodridge, Jeremy Hubbard, Bernie McGee, Fiona Hawkins, Becca Harvey, Susanne Masters, Jane Sendall, Hester Cox and Brian Stallwood, Anna Deacon, Nina Caudrey, Emma Norton, Kiara Henderson, Sam Lyon, Annie Dunford, Michael Balmain, David Weekes and Grahame Connor.

I want to thank my husband, Alastair, for all his help and support as my chief lifeguard, photographer, driver, camp-setter-upper and coffee and cake tester for my early research trips. I would also like to thank my other awesome research trip buddies – Jeremy Hubbard, Becca Harvey, and Fiona and Phil Hawkins – for battling rain, hail and wind, enduring soggy swims and missed ferries, and being enthusiastic cafe, bakery and pie shop testers.

A big thank you to Sian Jenkins for giving me the initial nudge I needed and to Kirsty Reade and the fantastic team at Vertebrate Publishing for their patience and expertise through the research and production process and for giving me the opportunity to write this book.

Thank you!

The swim spots: Alice's top fives

Top five river swim spots
1 River Etive *p22*
2 Linn of Dee *p116*
3 Soldier's Leap, Killiecrankie *p122*
4 Linn of Quoich *p118*
5 Glen Rosa, Arran *p2*

Top five waterfall swim spots
1 Eas Chia-aig Waterfall *p26*
2 Falls of Falloch *p126*
3 Lower Pattack Falls *p102*
4 River Etive *p22*
5 Fairy Pools, Skye *p34*

Top five freshwater lochs for swimming
1 Loch an Eilein *p98*
2 Loch Beinn a' Mheadhoin *p91*
3 Loch Maree *p62*
4 Loch Ness *p93*
5 Loch of the Lowes *p151*

Top five beaches for swimming
1 West Beach, Berneray *p48*
2 St Ninian's Beach, Shetland *p82*
3 Torastan Beach, Coll *p18*
4 Cullykhan Bay *p110*
5 Achmelvich *p71*

Top five multi-dip swim spots
1 Easdale Slate Quarries *p10*
2 River Etive & Loch Etive *p22 & p24*
3 Eas Chia-aig Waterfall & Loch Arkaig *p26 & p28*
4 Hopeman & Clashach Cove *p106*
5 Fife Tidal Pools *p139*

Top five swim spots for longer swims
1 Camusdarach Beach *p31*
2 Reef Beach, Lewis *p53*
3 Loch Morlich *p96*
4 Balnakeil Beach, Durness *p76*
5 Loch Lubnaig *p129*

Top five swim spots with gently sloping entries (good for beginners)
1 Loch Achilty *p90*
2 Loch Morlich *p96*
3 Brora Beach *p86*
4 Loch Venachar *p130*
5 Uisken Beach, Mull *p12*

Top five swim spots with things to swim to (or around)
1 Loch an Eilein (castle) *p98*
2 Inganess, Orkney (shipwreck) *p81*
3 Seagull Island, Loch Leven (island) *p25*
4 Lochindorb (castle) *p94*
5 Loch Achilty (island) *p90*

Top five swim spots for snorkelling
1 Uisken Beach, Mull *p12*
2 Clachan Sands, North Uist *p46*
3 Claigan Coral Beach, Skye *p38*
4 Achmelvich *p71*
5 Sanna Bay, Ardnamurchan *p30*

Top five swim spots for wildlife watching
1 Ardtalla Beach, Islay *p8*
2 Tràigh an t-Suidhe, Iona *p14*
3 Skaw Beach, Unst *p84*
4 Brora Beach *p86*
5 Upper Loch Torridon *p59*

Top five swim spots with spectacular scenery
1 Loch Clair *p61*
2 Ord Beach, Skye *p33*
3 Upper Loch Torridon *p59*
4 River Etive *p22*
5 Loch Morlich *p96*

Top five swim spots with longer walks
1 Glen Rosa, Arran (2.5km) *p2*
2 Port Ban Beach, Iona (2.5km) *p14*
3 Loch Muick (2km) *p114*
4 Claigan Coral Beach, Skye (1.8km) *p38*
5 Talisker Bay, Skye (1.5km) *p36*

Top five swim spots with short walks/easy access
1 Loch of the Lowes *p151*
2 Uisken Beach, Mull *p12*
3 Loch Lubnaig *p129*
4 Loch Maree *p62*
5 Sorobaidh Bay, Tiree *p17*

Top five swim spots with good food and drink options nearby
1 Loch Insh *p100*
2 Dores Beach, Loch Ness *p93*
3 Sorobaidh Bay, Tiree *p17*
4 Loch Lubnaig *p129*
5 St Mary's Loch & Loch of the Lowes *p151*

Top five swim spots with campsites nearby
1 Torastan Beach, Coll *p18*
2 Reef Beach, Lewis *p53*
3 Loch Morlich *p96*
4 Calgary Bay, Mull *p16*
5 Horgabost Beach, Harris *p50*

Top five swim spots for winter ice
1 Loch Morlich *p96*
2 Loch Insh *p100*
3 Loch Achilty *p90*
4 Loch Ettrick *p154*
5 Lochindorb *p94*

Index